The Businessman's Guide
to Dealing with the
Federal Government

The Businessman's Guide to Dealing with the Federal Government

Drake Publishers, Inc.   New York

Published in 1973 by
Drake Publishers Inc.
381 Park Avenue South
New York, N.Y. 10016

Library of Congress Cataloging in Publication Data
The Businessman's guide to dealing with the Federal Government.
    1. Government purchasing—United States.
JK1673.B87   353.007'12   73–4668
ISBN 0–87749–499–1

Printed by arrangement with the United States Government Printing Office
Printed in the United States of America

CONTENTS

95142

INTRODUCTION

Many businessmen do not realize that each year the Federal Government enters into thousands of supply and construction contracts that may be performed by the small business firm. These contracts are executed by headquarters offices of Federal departments or agencies in Washington, D.C., or at agency field offices or related activities located throughout the United States.

Also, some business concerns, big or small, do not understand the purchasing methods used by the Government. Rather than become involved in what they may consider complex bidding procedures, they automatically exclude their companies from consideration as prospective Government suppliers.

This booklet explains Government procurement principles and programs (Part I), and identifies those Government departments and agencies with major purchasing activities (Parts II thru IV). A review of these programs and procedures will result in a better understanding of ways and means for business concerns to receive an equitable share of the Government's purchasing business.

Part V provides a description of the common pitfalls involved in the submission of bids and in contract administration. This Part is of interest to the regular Government supplier as well as to the business firm making its initial effort to obtain a Government contract.

Part VI describes the manner in which businessmen may participate in sales of Government surplus property, including disposals of strategic and critical materials from Government stockpiles. Appendix material includes illustrated forms which are commonly used in Government procurements.

PART 1
Government procurement principles and programs

BASIC PRINCIPLES OF GOVERNMENT PROCUREMENT

When a manufacturer buys for his own business, he is concerned with obtaining a quality product, prompt delivery, and the most value for his money. The Federal Government is interested in these same basic purchasing considerations, including the maintenance of favorable supplier relationships. There are, however, certain differences in principles and procedures. The Government usually buys for use and not resale. Government procurement is not motivated by profit; and Government procurement is subject to legal and budget restrictions designed to safeguard the expenditure of public funds.

COMPETITIVE BIDS AND QUALITY CONTROL

A basic principle in Government procurement is to give all known responsible suppliers an equal chance to compete for Government contracts. In order to do this, the Government publicizes its intentions to buy through advertisements and announcements in various media and by sending invitations for bids to business firms whose names are on applicable mailing lists. Bids are opened on the deadline date, and the lowest responsible bidder meeting the specifications is awarded the contract.

Ordinarily you don't have to bid on the entire quantity we want. Bid only on that quantity for which your productive capacity and financial resources are adequate. All deliveries must be made in accordance with the schedule set forth in the Invitation. Submit your bid in the number of copies stated in the Invitation so that it will reach the issuing Supply Center by the hour and date set for the bid opening. . . . Don't forget—bidding is competitive, so quote your best price!

That's all there is to it . . .

If the low bidder does not quote on the entire quantity in the Invitation, contracts go to those low bidders whose combined offerings meet full requirements, provided that their prices are reasonable.

A record of all bids and awards is always available for your inspection at the issuing office, and frequently may be found in trade papers and journals. Contracts in excess of $25,000 are also reported in the Commerce Business Daily and provide a valuable source of possible subcontracting opportunities for you.

In certain circumstances it is not practical, not economical, or not possible to obtain bids. In such instances, regulations permit the Government to negotiate for the items it intends to procure. Procurement by negotiation, or unadvertised procurement, is specifically limited to those situations listed on page 8.

Procurement by negotiation does not relieve the Government

procurement officer of his responsibility to secure competition whenever possible. Normally the procurement officer will contact several reliable suppliers and award the contract to the one whose price and delivery of a product conforming to specifications will result in the most value received by the Government.

Another basic principle in procurement is that all supplies, equipment, and commodities offered by a supplier must be inspected and accepted by the Government before payment of the invoice. Inspection and testing are necessary to determine whether the goods offered meet each technical requirement of the contract, particularly the governing specifications.

HOW YOU GET PAID

SHIP ON TIME
Ship promptly in accordance with your contract delivery schedule.

KNOW THE PAYMENT PROCEDURE
The payment procedures for Government contracts are quite efficient and simple. Note carefully whether your contract specifies: (a) inspection and acceptance at source; (b) inspection at source, acceptance at destination; or, (c) inspection and acceptance at destination. The payment procedures to be followed for each of these alternatives are spelled out in your contract. Follow them carefully.

BILL ACCURATELY
Government regulations which protect you as a taxpayer require that you, as a contractor, submit a bill that is accurate in all respects. Errors in billing cause delays in payment. Make certain that you mail your voucher to the office specified in your contract.

GET PAID PROMPTLY

Fulfill your obligations under the contract, know and follow the proper payment procedure, bill us accurately, and you will be paid promptly.

SPECIFICATIONS AND STANDARDS

The use of specifications and standards is another principle in Government procurement. Specifications provide clear and accurate descriptions of the product or service to be bought, and prescribe the minimum requirement for quality and construction of materials and equipment necessary for an acceptable product. Standards reduce to a minimum the number of qualities, sizes, colors, varieties, and types of materials and commodities being procured.

Adopted as standard are those items which provide the greatest utility and economy and which are best suited to satisfy the bulk of the Government's requirements, with due regard to commercial availability, adequate quality, and other related considerations. Other types of standards involve methods of testing certain products. Engineering standards deal with design, construction, use, maintenance, and related product characteristics.

When a standard is established, the specification used in procurement of the item involved is based on the types, colors, and sizes provided by the standard. Standards have been established for several hundred items in common use in the Government, such as desks, file cabinets, and batteries.

Specifications, as used in the bulk of Government purchases, are either Federal or military. Federal Specifications are promulgated by the General Services Administration (GSA) and cover a wide variety of items in common use among Federal agencies. Federal Specifications are recognized by prefixes of single letters or combinations of the same letter, such as Q, KK, or LLL. These letters are code letters for the Federal Procurement Group in which the product covered by the specification is categorized. Military specifications cover items which are primarily for use by the military services. The prefix MIL is used to identify military specifications—for example, Specification No. MIL-P-20087.

Other types of specifications which are limited as to effective duration or Government agency include Interim Federal, interim military, and departmental specifications.

The GSA booklet, "Guide to Specifications and Standards of the Federal Government," describes all types of Government specifications and standards, their development and use, and the benefits provided to both industry and Government. This booklet also contains information about obtaining copies of specifications and standards. "Guide to Specifications and Standards of the Federal Government" is available, without charge, from GSA Business Service Centers and field offices of the Department of Commerce and Small Business Administration.

STANDARDIZED PROCUREMENT FORMS

Standardized procurement forms are an important element in carrying out the Government's objective to permit all responsible suppliers an equal chance to bid on Government supply needs. Standard forms have been developed to cover most bid and contractual situations, and these forms are used by all Federal agencies.

Invitations for bids on supply items are normally issued on Standard Form 33, Solicitation, Offer, and Award, which consolidates the invitation for bids and the contract award. Standard Form 33A contains the terms and conditions of the invitation.

Construction contracts require different standard forms from those used in supply contracts. Standard Form 19, Invitation, Bid, and Award—Construction, Alteration, or Repair; and Standard Form 23, Construction Contract, are the principal forms used for construction; however, other forms may be used, depending upon the requirements of the contract.

The most important points for businessmen to remember about

7

standard forms are that it is necessary that forms be completely and properly filled in before forwarding to the bidding or contracting officer; that bid and contractual forms must be signed; and that forms are often supported by additional conditions, some of which are incorporated by reference. For example, Standard Form 33 references the general contract provisions contained in Standard Form 32. The general provisions cover such subjects as inspection requirements, variations in quantity, payments, and contingent fees.

Standard forms commonly used in Government procurement are illustrated in the Appendix.

NEGOTIATED PURCHASES

Government procurement is not always conducted through formally advertised bids. Depending upon circumstances, procurement may be conducted by negotiation. Federal agencies are authorized to negotiate purchases:

If determined to be necessary during the period of a national emergency declared by the President or by the Congress. When the public exigency will not admit of the delay incident to advertising. When the purchase is under $2,500. For personal or professional services. For services rendered by educational institutions. For property or services to be procured and used outside the United States and its possessions. For medicines or medical property. For perishable or nonperishable subsistence supplies. For property purchased for authorized resale.

When it is impractical to secure competition, for example, when there is only one source of supply. Upon determination by the agency head that the items are for experimental, developmental, or research purposes. For purchases of items or services which the agency head determines should not be publicly disclosed because of their character, ingredients, or components.

For equipment which the agency head determines to be technical equipment, and in the public interest is necessary for assuring standardization and interchangeability of parts. When the agency head determines that the bid prices on advertised property or services are unreasonable, or have not been independently arrived at in open competition. When otherwise authorized by law. These criteria apply equally to military and civil agency procurements. The Armed Services Procurement Regulation includes additional criteria to cover certain military requirements, such as purchases in the interest of national defense or industrial mobilization.

CONSOLIDATED PURCHASE PROGRAMS

Even as large business corporations have found it advisable to separate overall operations into smaller and more workable branches, so the Federal Government has had to divide its procurement functions and make each agency responsible for most of its own procurement. However, continuous effort is being made to consolidate procurement functions, when consolidation is feasible and beneficial.

A major consolidation was made when the General Services Administration was established by passage of the Federal Property and Administrative Services act of 1949 (63 Stat. 377). This Act made GSA responsible for centralized procurement, storage, and distribution of supply items in common use throughout the Government. This action paved the way for more efficient and economical procurement of a vast quantity of items which previously were being purchased by individual agencies.

The military services have made steady progress in consolidating procurement programs, beginning with Single Department Procurement, under which the service with the predominant interest and experience buys a particular commodity for all three services.

In order to further consolidate total military needs for selected commodities, the Department of Defense established Single Managers. Single Managers were made responsible for determining requirements for all military services and for procurement, storage, and distribution to the services. For example, the Single Manager for electronics buys and distributes electronic supplies to the Army, Navy, and Air Force

Single Department Procurement differs from the Single Manager program in that the service responsible for procurement under the Single Department program does not determine requirements, manage inventories, or control issues.

Expanding on its consolidated procurement programs, the Department of Defense established the Defense Supply Agency (DSA) in 1961. DSA became responsible for all Single Managers (redesignated Defense Supply Centers) and other Department of Defense supply programs.

Although the Single Department Procurement program and Defense Supply Centers account for a substantial dollar volume of purchases, the major portion of military procurement is made by individual bureaus and commands of the three services.

Current agreements between GSA and the Department of Defense have resulted in a substantial number of items being purchased by military activities from GSA supply sources. Items purchased from GSA include such common-use ones as automotive equipment, household and office furniture, office supplies, paints, office machines, brushes, janitorial supplies, and hand tools.

REGULATIONS GOVERNING PROCUREMENT AND PROPERTY MANAGEMENT

Regulations with general applicability to agency procurement and supply programs are promulgated by GSA in the Federal Procurement Regulations (FPR) and the Federal Property Management Regulations (FPMR). The Armed Services Procurement Regulation is included in this section because military activities contract for the major portion of the Government's requirements. A brief description of each of these regulations i s presented in the following paragraphs.

FEDERAL PROCUREMENT REGULATIONS

The Federal Procurement Regulations contain uniform policies and procedures applicable to procurement by executive agencies of personal property and nonpersonal services, including construction.

These regulations are prescribed by the Administration of General Services and are published in the daily issue of the Federal Register. The regulations are also published in cumulative form in the Code of Federal Regulations.

Agencies are given an opportunity to comment on a proposed Federal Procurement Regulation, prior to its issuance, through the Interagency Procurement Policy Committee which serves as a media for coordinating such comments. Interested industrial or commercial organizations are also given an opportunity to comment when appropriate.

ARMED SERVICES PROCUREMENT REGULATION

Compatible with the Federal Procurement Regulations is the Armed Services Procurement Regulation, frequently referred to as the ASPR. The ASPR is issued by the Assistant Secretary of Defense (Installations and Logistics) and establishes for the Department of Defense uniform policies and procedures relating to the procurement of supplies and services under the authority of Chapter 137, Title 10, of the United States Code, or other statutory authority.

The Regulation is applicable to all military agencies and is published in the same manner as the Federal Procurement Regulations.

FEDERAL PROPERTY MANAGEMENT REGULATIONS

The Federal Property Management Regulations (FPMR) system is used by GSA to prescribe regulations, policies, procedures, and delegations of authority pertaining to the management of Government property and records, and other programs and activities of the type administered by GSA , except for procurement and contract matters contained in the Federal Procurement Regulations. FPMR issuances are published in the daily issue of the Federal Register, in cumulated form in the Code of Federal Regulations, and in separate loose-leaf volume form for distribution to Federal agencies.

These regulations are normally developed in coordination with other agencies, primarily those represented on the Interagency Committee for Improvement in Procurement and Management of Property, and with interested industrial or commercial concerns or organizations, and are promulgated by the Administrator of General Services.

AVAILABILITY OF REGULATIONS

The FPR and the FPMR are included in Title 41 of the Code of Federal Regulations as Chapter 1 and 101 respectively. The ASPR is included in Title 32 of the Code of Federal Regulations. The FPR and the ASPR may be ordered from the Superintendent of Documents, U.S. Government Printing Office, Washington, D.C. 20402. The FPMR is not generally available to the public as a separate publication. However, these regulations are published in the Federal Register which is available from the Superintendent of Documents.

SMALL BUSINESS ADMINISTRATION

The Small Business Administration was established in 1953 to assist the Nation's small business concerns. Major responsibilities of the Agency are: (1) To counsel with small business concerns on their financial problems; to help them obtain financing from private lending sources; and to make loans to them when private financing is not available on reasonable terms;

(2) To license, regulate, and help finance privately-owned small business investment companies, which in turn extend long-term and equity financing to small business concerns; (3) To make loans to state and local development companies to help them provide facilities for small businesses in their areas; (4) To make loans to help restore or replace businesses and homes damaged or destroyed by storms, floods and other disasters, including riots or civil disorders, and to assist small business concerns which have suffered subtantial economic injury because of drought or excessive rainfall; (5) To assist small firms in obtaining a fair share of Government prime and subcontracts, for supplies and services including research and development, and to help small business get a fair share of property being sold or leased by the Government; (6) To assist small firms in overcoming production problems, and in diversifying their product lines; (7) To assist small concerns with their management problems through training and counseling; (8) To help small concerns obtain the benefits or technological information resulting from research and development performed under Government contract or at Government expense; and (9) To provide detailed definitions of small businesses for use in identifying small business concerns to be assisted by the Agency and other Government offices having procurement, lending and other powers.

Complete information about SBA's various programs is available from the Agency's field offices, located in major cities.

The Small Bussiness Administration publishes a booklet that potential Government suppliers will find valuable—"U.S. Government Purchasing and Sales Directory." This publication contains a detailed listing of the products purchased by civilian and military Government agencies, locations of Government purchasing offices, and procedural information for use by suppliers, contractors and subcontractors in contract dealings with the U.S. Government. A complete listing of both military and civilian agencies and offices that contract for research and development with their fields of interest is given, together with a guide for submitting unsolicited proposals and suggestions for preparing brochures. It also contains a brief description of the Government's specifications system and explains how to obtain and use copies of Federal and military specifications. The Directory is available for reference at regional offices of the Small Business Administration. It is offered for sale at field offices of the U.S. Department of Commerce, and by the Superintendent of Documents, U.S. Government Printing Office, Washington, D.C. 20402.

DEPARTMENT OF COMMERCE PUBLICATIONS

COMMERCE BUSINESS DAILY

Every Monday through Friday the Department of Commerce publishes in the "Commerce Business Daily" a national list of U.S. Government proposed procurements, subcontracting leads, contract awards, sales of surplus property, and foreign business opportunities.

Publication of most of the listings in the "Commerce Business Daily" is required by law. In 1961, Congress directed the Secretary of Commerce to publish all procurement actions of $10,000 or more by military agencies and $5,000 or more by civil agencies. Exceptions are those procurements which are: (1) classified for reasons of national security; (2) perishable subsistence; (3) certain utility services; (4) required within 15 days; (5) placed under existing contracts; (6) made from other Government agencies; (7) personal professional services; (8) services from educational institutions; (9) made only from foreign sources; or (10) not to be given advance publicity, as approved by the Small Business Administration.

The "Commerce Business Daily" is available by subscription for $15 per year for regular mail and $52 per year additional for airmail. Orders should be sent to the Superintendent of Documents, U.S. Government Printing Office, Washington, D.C. 20402, or field offices of the Department of Commerce.

INTERNATIONAL COMMERCE

This weekly news magazine is the principal Commerce Department publication dealing with international trade. It gives concise, up-to-date information on trade and investment around the world—with a special section on business leads: Export, import, agency, and investment opportunities.

Regular departments cover trade fairs and trade center shows; business trends and economic conditions by country and area; and U.S. and foreign government actions affecting trade. Sample copies may be obtained from Commerce Department field offices on request.

Annual subscriptions to "International Commerce" are available for $20. Checks or money orders should be made payable to "Superintendent of Documents," and sent to the Superintendent of Documents, U.S. Government Printing Office, Washington, D.C. 20402.

WHO CONTRACTS FOR GOVERNMENT SUPPLY NEEDS

Government Buying Programs Can Be Divided Into Three Broad Categories:

MILITARY PROCUREMENT

Each department buys items that are peculiar to its own needs. Products that are general purpose, or common to two or more military services, are included under Defense Supply Agency procurement programs or are requisitioned from established Government sources of supply. Requirements for distribution through the supply system of each service are generally consolidated and procurement is made at central locations. However, local procurement under a certain dollar limitation is authorized for most military installations throughout the United States.

GSA PROCUREMENT

GSA procures, stores, and issues those items which are in general use by Government agencies, through the facilities of its depot system; procures general purpose items under Federal Supply Schedule term contracts for direct delivery to the using agency; and consolidates agency requirements for like items and secures quantity discounts under definite quantity contracts. GSA also makes purchases for individual requirements of agencies, upon their request, for direct delivery.

OTHER CIVIL AGENCY PROCUREMENT

Most civil agencies have their own procurement activities and buy from industry as well as established Government sources. Generally, the agency's open-market purchases are for items peculiar to its own needs, which often represent the predominant dollar value of its procurement expenditures.

These three categories are discussed in Parts 2, 3, and 4.

PART 2
Military
procurement

MILITARY PROCUREMENT PROGRAMS

The procurement responsibilities of the Army, Navy (including the Marine Corps), Air Force, and Defense Supply Agency are based upon providing supplies and services for the support of military operations. Although the largest percentage of the military budget is spent for aircraft, missiles, ships, tanks, and other capital equipment, the largest percentage of items is represented by spare parts, electronic equipment, and general purpose items required to maintain the active status of military installations. It is this latter category that provides the major potential for contracts for small business firms.

Military supply requirements are obtained under four primary programs: (1) procurement by the separate services under their own programs; (2) procurement from consolidated military sources, such as the Defense Supply Agency; (3) procurement from other Government sources, principally GSA; and (4) procurement from local sources of supply.

This booklet will not attempt to itemize the variety of items being procured by the various military services. Specific information about products bought by the military services and by agencies of the Department of Defense is available in the publication, "Selling to the Military," which contains an alphabetical listing of these products, and also gives the addresses of military procurement offices. Copies of "Selling to the Military" are available from the Superintendent of Documents, U.S. Government Printing Office, Washington, D.C. 20402, and from the military services.

Brief outlines of the major procurement programs of the Army, Navy, Air Force, and Defense Supply Agency are given on the following pages.

DEPARTMENT OF DEFENSE

The Department of Defense was created to provide unified direction of the three military services, to integrate policies and procedures which would result in coordinated military operations, and to establish a defense program which would provide the maximum national security.

The Office of the Secretary of Defense does not contract for any military supplies. These contracts are made by the individual military departments and Defense agencies, either for their own needs or for the combined needs of Department of Defense activities.

The Assistant Secretary of Defense for Installations and Logistics advises and assists the Secretary in the formulation of general policies in the fields of procurement, production, distribution, transportation, communications, and mobilization planning. From this office comes the policy guidance which shapes the development of each military service procurement system; which governs day-to-day relationships between the military procurement organizations; and which coordinates major procurement activities.

Military procurement polices and procedures authorized by

Title 10 of the United States Code are contained in the Armed Services Procurement Regulation. This regulation is further implemented by each of the military departments in their respective manuals and publications.

Each of the military services has small business specialists, located at major procurement activities. These specialists will gladly furnish complete information on how to do business with the agencies in the Department of Defense.

DEPARTMENT OF THE ARMY

The Department of the Army procurement organizations are commodity oriented at decentralized locations within the United States.

The Army Materiel Command has responsibility for the major part of the research and development and materiel procurement functions in support of the Army combat mission. Summarized below are brief descriptions of the missions of each subcommand and types of materiel they procure:

U.S. Army Missile Command, Redstone, Alabama
Rockets, guided missiles, ballistic missiles and support equipment.

U.S. Army Munitions Command, Dover, New Jersey
Integrated commodity management of nuclear and non-nuclear ammunition, rocket and missile warheads, chemical, biological, radiological material, fuzes, and propellants.

U.S. Army Aviation Systems Command, St. Louis, Missouri
Integrated commodity management of aeronautical and air delivery equipment and of test equipment that is part of or used with assigned material.

U.S. Army Electronics Command, Fort Monmouth, New Jersey

Communications, electronic intelligence gear, radio, radar, fire control systems, data processing devices, electronic test devices and related items.

U.S. Army Tank-Automotive Command, Warren, Michigan
Integrated commodity management of tactical wheeled and general purpose vehicles and related equipment.

U.S. Army Weapons Command, Rock Island, Illinois
Commodity management of weapons including artillery weapons, crew-served weapons, aricraft weapons systems, combat vehicles and related equipment.

U.S. Army Mobility Equipment Command, St. Louis, Missouri
Integrated commodity management of surface transportation equipment (other than tactical wheeled and general purpose vehicles); mapping and geodesy equipment; assigned electric power generation equipment; construction and services equipment; bridging equipment and related supplies.

U.S. Army Sentinel Logistics Command, Huntsville, Alabama
Provides mission essential logistic support to the Sentinel System except for nuclear munitions and auxiliary equipment.

U.S. Army Test and Evaluation Command, Aberdeen Proving Ground, Maryland
Conducts tests of materiel intended for use by the U.S. Army . Procurement limited to items required for use at the activity.

The Army Materiel Command also has procurement agencies located in New York, Chicago, Cincinnati, Los Angeles and San Francisco, in addition to a depot complex located throughout the United States. These activities procure many of the items purchased by the major commodity commands.

The U.S. Army Corps of Engineers is responsible for

contracting for military construction, repair of buildings, structures maintenance, and civil works, such as river and harbor improvement, flood control and related projects.

Purchases at posts, camps, hospitals, and similar installations are generally less complex than those at the commodity commands. Usually purchases consist of items needed in direct support of the mission at the activity.

Detailed information about Army procurement is contained in the Department of Defense publication "Selling to the Military." Information concerning the commodity commands of the Army Materiel Command is contained in the "Contractors Guide" available at major Army purchasing offices.

DEPARTMENT OF THE NAVY

The Department of the Navy is organized into four principal parts. These are: (1) the operating forces, composed of the Office of the Chief of Naval Operations, the seagoing forces, including the Fleet Marine Forces and such other Navy field activities and commands as assigned by the Secretary of the Navy; (2) the U.S. Marine Corps, within the Department of the Navy, which includes Headquarters, U.S. Marine Corps, the operating forces of the Marine Corps, and the Marine Corps supporting establishments; (3) the Naval Material Command, which includes Headquarters Naval Material Command and the following functional commands: Naval Air Systems Command, Naval Electronic Systems Command, Naval Facilities Engineering Command, Naval Ordnance Systems Command, Naval Ship Systems Command, and the Naval Supply Systems Command, and field activities as assigned by the Secretary of the Navy; (4) other supporting organizations, which include the Bureau of Naval Personnel, Bureau of Medicine and Surgery, the Office of the Comptroller of the Navy, Office of the Judge Advocate General, Office of Naval Research, offices of staff assistants and the shore activities as assigned by the Secretary of the Navy.

Under the supervision and guidance of the Assistant Secretary of the Navy (Installations and Logistics), each Systems Command designs, procures, controls, and maintains the major items of equipment—ships, planes, missiles, guns, communication devices, and construction equipment—needed by the operating forces. Because each Systems Command has a somewhat distinctive mission, there is little duplication accepted the management of these major supply items.

To support, operate, and maintain these major items of equipment requires about one and one-quarter million repair parts and expendable supplies, known as "secondary supply items." These items include common-use supplies such as spark plugs, tires, office supplies, keys, batteries—in short, everything from paper clips to video scanning tubes. These are the items of primary interest to the small businessman seeking a Government contract.

The Naval Supply Systems Command is responsible for the supply management of secondary supply items. This assignment provides for centralized control over purchasing, storage, issue, disposal, inventory control, cataloging, and traffic management for the vast number of common-use items required by naval activities.

Inventory Control Points are the nerve centers of the Navy supply system. These offices are subject to general guidance of the Naval Supply Systems Command for supply and business management functions, with functions performed by technicians and engineers being under the guidance of the appropriate Systems Command. Inventory Control Points serve as inventory managers for secondary supply items. Except for those items now controlled by the Defense Supply Agency, Inventory Control Points determine how much to buy, when to buy, where to buy, and how to distribute to the point of use.

Distribution of supply items is made from strategically located Naval Supply Centers and Depots, directly to the operating forces and to elements of the shore establishment. The supply

24

departments of naval air stations, shipyards, ordnance plants, training centers, and other facilities draw upon the nearest supply center or depot for the bulk of their requirements, except for items authorized for local purchase or for purchase from GSA.

A detailed listing of Navy and Marine Corps purchasing offices is contained in the Department of Defense publication, "Selling to the Military."

DEPARTMENT OF THE AIR FORCE

Air Force procurement is carried out under three principal programs: (1) Systems Procurement, (2) Support Procurement, and (3) Base Procurement.

Systems Procurement covers the purchase of manual aircraft systems, missile systems, space systems, and communications systems. This program begins with initial development and continues until the systems are accepted into the Air Force inventory. This program is the responsibility of the Air Force Systems Command with headquarters at Andrews Air Force Base, Maryland.

Support Procurement consists of procurement of supplies and services required to support the weapons and communications systems after they have been accepted into the Air Force inventory. This procurement is the responsibility of the Air Force Logistics Command with headquarters at Wright-Patterson Air Force Base, Ohio.

Base Procurement (formerly called "local purchase") is performed by the more than 128 Air Force bases in the United States for hundreds of thousands of items needed in the daily operation of bases. Most of these items are obtained from local businesses or from regional offices of GSA. Items that are purchased locally are generally readily available on the open market; are less complex than those which are centrally procured; and are of a type more commercial than military. Base procurement includes supplies, equipment, minor construction, local repairs, and services of a "housekeeping" nature, as authorized under the base procurement program.

Businessmen interested in bidding on Air Force contracts for either systems or support procurement should first apply at the Defense Contract Administration Services Regional Office in their region. Each such office has a small business specialist to assist small businessmen.

DEFENSE SUPPLY AGENCY

When the Defense Supply Agency was established, the various Single Managers were consolidated and overall responsibility for their operation assigned to the military head of DSA. Single Managers were redesignated as Supply Centers, with the following now in operation:

Defense Personnel Support Center
Defense Fuel Supply Center
Defense General Supply Center
Defense Construction Supply Center
Defense Industrial Supply Center
Defense Electronics Supply Center

Each of the Defense Supply Centers has procurement responsibility for the commodities assigned to it. The Centers determine requirements, procure, store, and issue for the Armed Forces. Defense Supply Centers are located in various cities throughout the United States.

In addition to the commodity Supply Centers, DSA is responsible for the Defense Logistics Services Center, which handles the military programs for Federal cataloging, property utilization, and surplus property disposal. DSA is also

26

responsible for the Defense Documentation Center, which is a central facility for scientific and technical documentation and for secondary distribution of formally recorded research, development, test, and evaluation results from the various components of DOD.

DSA administers procurement contracts through its Defense Contract Administration Services (DCAS) organization for the three military departments, DSA, NASA, for other Federal and State agencies and, when authorized, for foreign governments. Previously, the military departments and other agencies managed their own contracts. A few categories of contracts such as the major weapons systems, large civil works construction and shipbuilding continue to be administered by the military departments. DSA is also responsible for the Defense Industrial Plant Equipment Center, which handles the development and maintenance of central records of the Defense Department's inventory of industrial plant equipment, and the management of idle equipment.

LABOR SURPLUS AREAS and/or CERTIFIED-ELIGIBLE FIRMS

It is the policy of the Department of Defense to aid firms in labor surplus areas and other certified-eligible firms.

In order to carry out this policy, a part of a procurement may be set aside for negotiation with concerns which are certified-eligible or which will perform, or cause to be performed, in a labor surplus area , a substantial portion of the contracts thus awarded.

This is an important preference for companies which qualify.

The Small Business and Economic Utilization Specialist at each Buying Office and at each DCAS Office can explain this preference to you and help you participate in DSA procurements. Consult him.

SUBCONTRACTING

One of the greatest opportunities small business firms have for participating in Department of Defense business, other than contracting directly with a Defense Agency, is by subcontracting with firms that have Department of Defense contracts. Opportunities in the subcontracting field are often overlooked by small business firms.

Department of Defense contracts in the amount of $500,000 or more, having substantial subcontracting possibilities, require that the contractor maintain a Defense Small Business Subcontracting and Labor Surplus Area Program. Such contractors are required to designate a Small Business Liaison Officer who administers the company subcontracting program. These programs are designed to assist small business firms and to afford them opportunities to participate in Defense work as subcontractors. The Commerce Business Daily is useful in identifying firms which offer subcontracting opportunities.

THE DSA INDUSTRIAL MOBILIZATION PROGRAM

Total national defense requires that we look closely at the plans for supporting our military forces during any future emergency. We must be assured that, should such an emergency arise, the industrial resources of the country will be able to provide prompt and effective support for our military needs.

In order to achieve this goal, we are continually working out arrangements with manufacturers who agree to take certain actions immediately upon declaration of an emergency. These actions, planned in advance, are designed to reduce the time period that normally elapses before a manufacturer receives an order and goes into production.

We have already developed such plans with several thousand manufacturers. We would like to explore with you your

28

possibilities for joining us in this essential defense work. If you are interested in this program, contact the nearest DSA Supply Center or Defense Contract Administration Service Office.

DEFENSE PRIORITIES AND ALLOCATION PROGRAM

In order to assure timely deliveries of material and equitable distribution of controlled materials, the Defense Production Act of 1950 authorizes the Department of Defense to assign priority ratings or material allotments to most of its contracts. Your subcontractors will deliver supplies, components, and material to you and to their other customers according to the priorities governing the orders they receive. You must therefore include the rating or allotment assigned to your contract in your subcontracts to assure that your requirements are given the proper precedence of delivery. If any problems arise in this area, you should contact the DCAS office or the Contracting Officer.

AN ALPHABETICAL LISTING OF COMMODITIES PURCHASED BY THE DEFENSE SUPPLY AGENCY

Commodities	Centers
A	
Accessories, Machine Tool	G
Accessories for Secondary Metal-working Machinery	G
Air Conditioning Equipment	G
Air Purification Equipment	C
Alarm and Signal Systems, Miscellaneous	G
Antennas, Waveguides, and Related Equipment	E

Commodities	Centers
** Architectural and Related Metal Products	C
Armor, Personal	PT

B

Commodities	Centers
Badges and Insignia	PT
** Bags and Sacks	G
Bakery and Cereal Products	PS
Ballasts, Lampholders, and Starters	G
Bars and Rods, Iron and Steel	I
Bars and Rods, Nonferrous Base Metal	I
Batteries, Secondary	G
Bearings, Antifriction, Unmounted	I
Bearings, Mounted	I
Bearings, Plain, Unmounted	I
Belting, Drive Belts, Fan Belts and Accessories	C
Beverages, Nonalcoholic	PS
Blocks, Tackle, Rigging, and Slings	I
Bolts	I
Books and Pamphlets	G
Bottles and Jars	G
** Boxes, Cartons, and Crates	G
** Building Glass, Tile, Brick, and Block	C

C

Commodities	Centers
** Cabinets, Lockers, Bins, and Shelving	G
Cable, Cord, and Wire Assemblies: Communication Equipment	G

Commodities	Centers
Cameras, Motion Picture	G
Cameras, Still Picture	G
Capacitors	E
Centrifugals, Separators, and Pressure and Vacuum Filters	C
Chain and Wire Rope	I
Chemical Analysis Instruments	PM
*** Chemical Specialties, Miscellaneous	F & G
*** Chemicals	F & G
Children's and Infants' Apparel and Accessories	PT
Circuit Breakers	E
Clean Work Stations, Controlled Environment, & Related Equipment	G
Clothing, Special Purpose	PT
Coffee, Tea, and Cocoa	PS
Coil, Flat & Wire Springs	I
Coils and Transformers	E
Communication Equipment, Miscellaneous	E
Compressors and Vacuum Pumps	C
Condiments and Related Products	PS
Connectors, Electrical	E
Construction Equipment, Miscellaneous	C
** Construction Materials, Miscellaneous	C
** Containers, Utility, Household and Commercial	G
Converters, Electrical Non-Rotating	G

31

Commodities	Centers
Converters, Electrical Rotating	G
Conveyors	C
Cosmetics and Toiletries, Medicated	PM
Crane and Crane-Shovel Attachments	C
Cranes and Crane-Shovels	C
** Cutlery and Flatware	G
Cutting Tools for Machine Tools	G
Cutting & Forming Tools for Secondary Metalworking Machinery	G

D

Commodities	Centers
Dairy Foods and Eggs	PS
Dental Instruments, Equipment, & Supplies	PM
Drafting, Surveying, and Mapping Instruments	G
Driers, Dehydrators, and Anhydrators	C
Drugs, Biologicals, & Official Reagents	PM
Drums and Cans	G
Dyes	G

E

Commodities	Centers
Earth Moving and Excavating Equipment	C
Ecclesiastical Equipment, Furnishings, and Supplies	G
Electric Arc Welding Equipment	G
Electric Lamps	G

Commodities	Centers
Electric Portable and Hand Lighting Equipment	G
Electric Power and Distribution Equipment, Miscellaneous	G
Electric Vehicular Lights and Fixtures	G
Electrical and Electronic Components, Miscellaneous	E
Electrical Contact Brushes and Electrodes	G
Electrical Control Equipment	G
Electrical Hardware and Supplies	G
Electrical Insulators and Insulating Materials	G
Engine Accessories, Nonaircraft, Miscellaneous	C
Engine Air and Oil Filters, Strainers, and Clearners, Nonaircraft	C
Engine Cooling System Components, Nonaircraft	C
Engine Electrical System Components, Nonaircraft	C
Engine Fuel System Components, Nonaircraft	C
Engines and Components, Diesel	C
Engines and Components, Miscellaneous	C
Engines, Gasoline, Reciprocating, Except Aircraft; and Components	C

F

Fabricated Materials, Nometallic, Miscellaneous	G

Commodities	Centers
Fans, Air Circulators, and Blower Equipment	G
Fastening Devices	I
Fencing, Fences, and Gates	C
Fibers: Vegetable, Animal, & Synthetic	PT
Filing Machines	G
Filters and Networks	E
Fire Fighting Equipment	C
Fittings for Rope, Cable, and Chain	I
Fittings and Specialties: Hose, Pipe, and Tube	C
Flags and Pennants	PT
Flight Clothing and Accessories, Specialized	PT
Food Cooking, Baking, and Serving Equipment	G
Food Oils and Fats	PS
Food Packages, Composite	PS
Food Preparation and Serving Sets, Kits, and Outfits	G
Foods, Special Dietary and Food Specialty Preparations	PS
Footwear, Men's	PT
Footwear, Women's	PT
Forging Machinery and Hammers	G
Foundary Machinery Related Equipment & Supplies	G
Fruits and Vegetables	PS
Fuel Burning Equipment Units	C
Fuel Oils	F

Commodities	Centers
Fuels, Solid	F
Fur Materials	PT
Furnishings, Household	PT
** Furniture, Household	G
** Furniture, Office	G
** Furniture and Fixutres, Miscellaneous	G
Fuses and Lightning Arresters	E

G

Gas Cylinders, Commercial and Industrial	G
Gas Generating and Dispensing Systems, Fixed or Mobile	G
Gases: Compressed and Liquefield	G
Gears, Pulleys, Sprockets, and Transmission Chain	C
Generators and Generator Sets, Electrical	G
Glass Fabricated Materials	G

H

Hardware, Miscellaneous	I
Harvesting Equipment	C
Headsets, Handsets, Microphones and Speakers	E
Heating Equipment, Space; Domestic Water Heaters	C
Hides; Miscellaneous Crude Animal Products	PT
Hose and Tubing, Flexible	C
Hosiery, Handwear, and Clothing Accessories, Men's	PT

35

Commodities	Centers
Hosiery, Handwear, and Clothing Accessories, Women's	PT
Hospital and Surgical Clothing and Textile Special Purpose Items	PT
Hospital Furniture, Equipment, Utensils, and Supplies	PM

I

Commodities	Centers
Individual Equipment	PT
Industrial Sewing Machines and Mobile Textile Repair Shops	G
Instruments, Comination & Miscellaneous	G
Instruments, Geophysical and Astronomical	G
Instruments Measuring, Liquid and Gas Flow, Liquid Level, and Mechanical Motion	G
Instruments, Measuring & Testing, Electrical & Electronic Properties	E
Instruments, Meteorological and Apparatus	G
Instruments, Pressure Temperature & Humidity Measuring & Controlling	G
Instruments, Time Measuring	G
Intercommunication and Public Address Systems, Airborne	E
Intercommunication and Public Address Systems, except Airborne	E

J

Commodities	Centers
Jams, Jellies, and Preserves	PS

Commodities	Centers
K	
Kitchen Equipment and Appliances	G
** Kitchen Hand Tools and Utensils	G
Knobs and Pointers	I
L	
Laboratory Equipment and Supplies	PM
Lathes	G
Laundry and Dry Cleaning Equipment	G
Leather	PT
Lifesaving and Diving Equipment, Marine	C
Lighting Fixtures, Indoor and Outdoor Electric	G
Lighting Fixtures, Nonelectric	G
Lubrication and Fuel Dispensing Equipment	C
Luggage	PT
Lugs, Terminals, and Terminal Strips	G
Lumber and Related Basic Wood Materials	C
M	
Machinery, Chemical and Pharmaceutical Products	G
Machinery, Crystal and Glass Industries	G
Machinery, Industrial Size Reduction	G
Machinery, Rubber and Plastic Working.	G

Commodities	Centers
Machinery, Sawmill and Planing Mill	G
Machinery, Special Industry, Miscellaneous	G
Machinery, Specialized Metal Container Manufacturing & Related Equipment	G
Machines, Bending and Forming	G
Machines, Boring	G
Machines, Broaching	G
Machines, Drilling & Tapping	G
Machines, Electric & Ultrasonic Erosion	G
Machines, Gear Cutting and Finishing	G
Machines, Grinding	G
Machines, Industrial Assembly	G
Machines, Industrial Marking	G
Machines, Metal Forming and Cutting, Miscellaneous, Secondary	G
Machines, Milling	G
Machines, Punching and Shearing	G
Machines, Rolling Mills and Drawing	G
Machines, Riveting	G
Machine Shop Sets, Kits, and Outfits	G
Machine Tools, Miscellaneous	G
Machine Tools, Portable	G
Machines, Wire and Metal Ribbon Forming	G
Machines, Woodworking	G

Commodities	Centers
Machining Centers & Way-Type Machines	G
Materials Handling Equipment, Miscellaneous	G
Materials Handling Equipment, Nonself- Propelled	G
Meat, Poultry, and Fish	PS
Medical and Surgical Instruments, Equipment, and Supplies	PM
Medical Sets, Kits, and Outfits	PM
Metal Finishing Equipment	G
Metal Heat Treating Equipment	G
Microelectronic Circuit Devices	E
Millwork	C
** Mineral Construction Materials, Bulk	C
Minerals, Natural and Synthetic	F
Mining, Rock Drilling, Earth Boring, and Related Equipment	C
Miscellaneous Crude Animal Products, Inedible	PT
Miscellaneous Item	G
Mortuary Supplies	G
Motors, Electrical	G
Music, Sheet and Book	G

N

Nails, Keys, and Pins	I
Notions and Apparel Findings	PT
Nuts and Washers	I

O

Oils and Greases: Cutting, Lubricating, and Hydraulic	F

Commodities	Centers
Opticians' Instruments, Equipment, and Supplies	PM
Outerwear, Men's	PT
Outerwear, Women's	PT
P	
Packing and Gasket Materials	I
Padding and Staffing Materials	PT
** Paper and Paperboard	G
Pest Control Agents and Disinfectants	G
Pest, Disease, and Frost Control Equipment	C
Petroleum Production and Distrubution Equipment	C
Photographic Developing and Finishing Equipment	G
Photographic Equipment & Accessories	G
Photographic Projection Equipment	G
Photographic Supplies	G
Phhysical Properties Testing Equipment	G
Piezoelectric Crystals	E
Pipe and Tube	C
Planers and Shapers	G
Plastics Fabricated Materials	G
Plate, Sheet, Strip, and Foil: Nonferrous Base Metal	I
Plate, Sheet, Strip, Foil and Wire: Precious Metal	I
Plate, Sheet, and Strip: Iron and Steel	I

Commodities	Centers
Plumbing Fixtures and Accessories	C
Plumbing, Heating and Sanitation Equipment, Miscellaneous	C
Plywood and Veneer	C
Power Transmission Equipment, Miscellaneous	C
Prefabricated and Portable Buildings	C
Prefabricated Structures, Miscellaneous	C
Presses, Hydraulic and Pneumatic, Power-driven	G
Presses, Manual	G
Presses, Mechanical Power Driven	G
Printed Matter, Miscellaneous	G
Printing, Duplicating and Bookbinding Equipment	G
Production Jigs, Fixtures, and Templates	G
Propellants and Fuels, Liquid, Petroleum Base	F
Pumps, Power and Hand	C

Q

None

R

Radio & Television Communication Equipment, Airborne	E
Radio & Television Communication Equipment except Airborne	E
Radio Navigation Equipment, except Airborne	E
Refractories and Fire Surfacing Materials	G

Commodities	Centers
Refrigeration and Air Conditioning Components	G
Refrigeration Equipment	G
Relays, Contactors, and Solenoids	E
Resistors	E
Right-of-Way Construction and Maintenance Equipment, Railroad	C
Rings, Shims and Spacers	I
Rivets	I
Road Clearing and Cleaning Equipment	C
Rope, Cordage, and Twine	I
Rubber Fabricated Materials	G

S

Commodities	Centers
Saddlery, Harness, Whips, and Related Animal Furnishings	C
Safety & Rescue Equipment	G
Saws and Filing Machines	G
Sawmill and Planing Mill Machinery	G
Scaffolding Equipment and Concrete Forms	C
Scales and Balances	G
Screening, Metal	I
Screws	I
Semiconductor Devices and Associated Hardware	E
Semiconductor, Specialized, Microelectronic Circuit Device & Printed Circuit Board Manufacturing Machinery	G
Sewage Treatment Equipment	C
Shims, Spacers and Rings	I

Commodities	Centers
Shoe Findings and Soling Materials	PT
Shoe Repairing Equipment	G
** Signs, Advertising Displays, and Identification Plates	G
Soil Preparation Equipment	C
S ound Recording and Reproducing Equipment	E
Soups and Bouillons	PS
Space Heating Equipment and Domestic Water Heaters	C
Springs, Coil, Flat and Wire	I
** Stationery and Record Forms	G
Storage Tanks	C
Structural Shapes, Iron and Steel	I
Structural Shapes, Nonferrous Base Metal	I
Studs	I
Sugar, Confectionery, and Nuts	PS
Surgical Dressing Materials	PM
Switches	E
Synchros and Resolvers	E

T

Commodities	Centers
** Tableware	G
Teletype and Facsimile Equipment	E
Telephone and Telegraph Equipment	E
Tents and Tarpaulins	PT
Textile Fabrics	PT
Tobacco Products	PS
Tools and Attachments for woodworking Machinery	G
* Tools, Measuring; Sets, Kits, and Outfits	G

Commodities	Centers
Torque Converters & Speed Changers	C
Tractors, Full Track, Low Speed	C
Tractors, Wheeled	C
Transformers: Distribution and Power Station	G
Trucks and Tractor Attachments	C
Trucks and Tractors, Self-Propelled, Warehouse	C
Tubes: Electron and associated Hardware	E

U

Underwear and Nightwear, Men's	PT
Underwear and Nightwear, Women's	PT

V

Valves, Nonpowered	C
Valves, Powered	C
Vehicular Brake, Steering, Axle, Wheel, and Track Components	C
Vehicular Cab, Body, and Frame Structural Components	C
Vehicular Components, Miscellaneous	C
Vehicular Furniture and Accessories	C
Vehicular Power Transmission Components	C

W

Water Distillation Equipment, Marine and Industrial	C
Water Purification Equipment	C
Waxes, Oils, and Fats, Miscellaneous	F

Commodities	Centers
Welding Equipment, Gas, Heat Cutting and Metalizing	G
Welding Equipment, Electric ARC	G
Welding Equipment Electric Resistance	G
Welding Positioners and Manipulators	G
Welding Equipment, Miscellaneous	G
Welding Supplies & Equipment, Miscellaneous Soldering & Brazing	G
Winches, Hoists, Cranes, and Derricks	C
Wire and Cable, Electrical	I
Wire, Nonelectrical, Iron and Steel	I
Wire, Nonelectrical, Nonferrous Base Metal	I
Woodworking Machines	G

X

X-Ray Equipment and Supplies: Medical, Dental, Veterinary	PM

Y

Yarn and Thread	PT

DSA—GUIDE FOR PROCUREMENTS:

DSA procurements are accomplished by six (6) Defense Supply Centers. Small Business Specialists are available at the Centers to assist businessmen in their efforts to sell to DSA. The telephone numbers listed below are those of the Specialists.

C   Defense Construction Supply
Center
3990 East Broad Street
Columbus, Ohio 43215
Tel: A.C. 614; 236-3541

E   Defense Electronics Supply Center
1507 Wilmington Pike
Dayton, Ohio 45401
Tel: A.C. 513; 252-5231

F   Defense Fuel Supply Center
Cameron Station, Bldg. 8
5010 Duke Street
Alexandria, Virginia 22314
Tel: A.C. 202; 274-7428

G   Defense General Supply Center
Bellwood, Petersburg Pike
Richmond, Virginia 23219
Tel: A.C. 703; 275-3617

I   Defense Industrial Supply Center
700 Robbins Avenue
Philadelphia, Pennsylvania 19111
Tel: A.C. 215; 697-2747

P   Defense Personnel Support Center
2800 South 20th Street
Philadelphia, Pennsylvania 19101
Tel: A.C. 215; 271-2321
PM-(Medical—Dental)
PS-(Subsistence)
PT-(Textiles and Clothing)

* GSA has purchase responsibility only for common commercial type items within this class.

** GSA has purchase responsibility within these classes except for limited number of items.

*** "F" has purchase responsibility for petroleum base items only.

PART 3
General
Services
Administration

GENERAL SERVICES ADMINISTRATION
REGIONAL OFFICES AND
BUSINESS SERVICE CENTERS

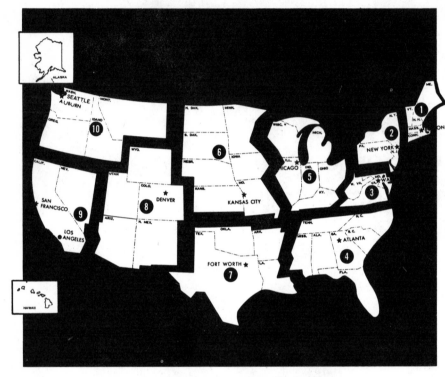

1. BOSTON, MASSACHUSETTS 02109
   Post Office and Courthouse
   BOSTON, MASSACHUSETTS 02203
 * John F. Kennedy Federal Building

2. NEW YORK, NEW YORK 10007
   26 Federal Plaza

3. WASHINGTON, D.C. 20407
   7th and D Streets, SW.

4. ATLANTA, GEORGIA 30309
   1776 Peachtree Street, NW.

5. CHICAGO, ILLINOIS 60604
   219 S. Dearborn Street

6. KANSAS CITY, MISSOURI 64131
   1500 E. Bannister Road

7. FT. WORTH, TEXAS 76102
   819 Taylor Street

8. DENVER, COLORADO 80225
   Building 41, Denver Federal Center

9. SAN FRANCISCO, CALIFORNIA 94103
   49 Fourth Street
 * LOS ANGELES, CALIFORNIA 90012
   300 N. Los Angeles Street

10. AUBURN, WASHINGTON 98002
    GSA Center
 * SEATTLE, WASHINGTON 98104
   909 First Avenue

*Business Service Centers other than those at regional offices.

GSA BUSINESS SERVICE CENTERS

In dealing with GSA, businessmen have the advantage of a central source of information for all GSA activities and operations in each major geographical area of the United States. GSA Business Service Centers have been established in each city in which there is a GSA regional office (except Auburn, Washington), for the specific purpose of providing service and assistance to business concerns interested in participating in Government procurement and disposal contracts. Business Service Centers have also been established in Los Angeles, California and Seattle, Washington.

GSA Business Service Centers advise businessmen of methods of doing business with the Government and provide information on: (1) Federal procurement and disposal policies, regulations and procedures for both real and personal property ; (2) bids and related documents; (3) specifications (4) contract forms and conditions; (5) quantities and prices of past contract awards; (6)

National Archives and Records Service

Procures commercial services in connection with programs for records management; selecting, preserving, and servicing Government records; and administering Presidential libraries.

Public Buildings Service

Acquires real property and constructs buildings for Government use. Buys necessary supplies and materials for repair, remodeling, and maintenance of Government buildings.

Federal Supply Service

Buys supplies and contracts for services for the common needs of all Government agencies. Makes special purchases for agency requirements upon their request or under special agreements.

Transportation and Communications Service

Contracts and negotiates for transportation, public utility, and communications services for Federal agencies. Operates the Federal Telecommunications System and Government motor pools.

Property Management and Disposal Service

Contracts for services related to rehabilitation, reclamation, utilization, and/or sale of in-use, excess, or surplus real and personal property, plus procurement and disposal of stockpile materials.

names of current prime contractors from ,whom subcontracts might be obtainable; and (7) other pertinent procurement and disposal information.

Business Service Centers also: display current bid invitations, bid tabulations, contract awards data and GSA catalogs; receive and safeguard bids submitted in response to GSA invitations until bid opening time; and furnish copies of Federal Supply Schedules, specifications, Federal regulations and procedures, standard contract forms and related forms and publications.

GSA PROCUREMENT PROGRAMS

The Government-wide procurement and supply responsibilities of GSA are carried out by the Federal Supply Service, Property Management and Disposal Service, Transportation and Communications Service, and Public Buildings Service, and are described in detail on the following pages. The basic procurement programs of these Services are outlined (see diagram on facing page), including reference to the National Archives and Records Service.

PROPERTY MANAGEMENT AND DISPOSAL SERVICE

The Property Management and Disposal Service (PMDS) of GSA has a two fold responsibility: (1) to manage the Nation's stockpile of strategic and critical materials, and (2) to dispose of excess and surplus supplies, equipment, and real property no longer needed by the Federal Government.

The disposal activities serve two major purposes: initially, available Government property is utilized among Government agencies in lieu of new procurement, thereby minimizing cash expenditures for new purchases; and obversely, maximizing cash returns to the Government by actual disposals of excess stockpile materials and the sale of other personal property and surplus real property.

STRATEGIC AND CRITICAL MATERIALS

The Strategic and Critical Materials Stock Piling Act provides for the acquisition and retention of strategic and critical materials and encourages the conservation and development of sources of materials within the United States, and thereby decreases and prevents a dangerous and costly dependence upon foreign nations for supplies of these materials in time of national emergency.

The Office of Emergency Preparedness (OEP) in the Executive Office of the President is responsible for determining the quantity, quality, and type of materials to be stockpiled. In making these determinations, the OEP utilizes the skills, knowledge, and services of other Government agencies, including GSA and the Departments of the Interior, Agriculture, Commerce, Defense, Treasury, and State. In addition, the advice and cooperation of industrial and commercial firms regarding the type, form, and quality of materials to be stockpiled, plus changes in materials and technology, has assisted in maintaining a utility of the stockpiled materials to meet the probable demands of a war-time economy.

There are 92 commodities in the total stockpile inventory; and 77 different metals, minerals, ores, and agricultural materials now have stockpile objectives. The total inventory has a current market value of approximately $6.8 billion as of April 1969.

GSA, under the provisions of the Defense Stockpile Act of 1950, is responsible for the acquisition of strategic metals, minerals, and other materials for Government use or resale. PMDS administers this major program and in addition promotes the expansion of commercial productive capacity and the supply of strategic and critical materials which serve to lessen dependency upon foreign sources of supply. Though it is Government policy to procure materials for the stockpile from

52

domestic sources whenever feasible, some materials are not available in this country and must be procured abroad. Purchases of materials are made on a competitive basis, or, when appropriate, by direct negotiations.

Purchase of storage aids necessary in the maintenance of stockpiled materials cover such items as pallets, polyethylene bags, galvanized steel drums, and burlap bags. When available, Government excess items are used. In addition, services related to the maintenance of the stockpile are bought. These services include materials handling, repackaging, sampling, analyzing, and services related to the upgrading of materials. Procurement is through publicly advertised bids, or, when appropriate, direct negotiation.

Further information about types of material and quantities procured is available from GSA Business Service Centers.

PERSONAL PROPERTY

Businessmen are afforded the opportunity to contract for maintenance, repair, rehabilitation, and reclamation of excess property.

The property rehabilitation program provides service-type contracts for such items as furniture, office machines, tires and tubes, refrigeration and air-conditioning equipment, household appliances, and fire extinguishers. Service contracts are currently in effect for the reclamation of precious metals such as platinum, irridium, and silver from used aircraft sparkplugs and magneto points; and the recovery of silver from used photographic fixing solution and scrap film. In most instances, Government agencies are authorized to place orders directly with the contractors.

Small business commercial contractors are the main suppliers of the above services; however, GSA utilizes the Federal Prison Industries, Inc., for furniture rehabilitation and the National Industries for the Blind for the renovation of cotton-felted mattresses.

GSA Business Service Centers can furnish information concerning bid procedures and specifications for rehabilitation services currently being solicited by and for the Government.

REAL PROPERTY

PMDS continually seeks persons interested in performing appraisal, auctioneer, broker, and other contract services for the Government, which are described below in detail. Interested persons should write to the nearest GSA regional office and request the necessary application forms. Approved applicants are eligible to receive invitations to submit proposals for rendering the requested services.

Appraisal

In leasing, buying, exchange, utilization, and disposal of real (and related personal) property, GSA employs its own staff, independent appraisal companies, and individuals to report the estimated fair market value or the estimated fair annual rental of the properties. A period of 30 to 90 days is usually required for appraisals though the actual time is dependent upon the size and complexity of the properties. Appraisers are selected from the GSA Register of Available Real Estate Appraisers for which a minimum of five years appraisal experience in commerical and industrial property fields is required.

Interested appraisers should write to the nearest GSA regional office and request GSA Form 1195, Application for Placement on GSA Register of Available Real Estate Appraisers. If approved, their names will be placed on the Register and they will be eligible to receive invitations to submit proposals for appraisal work in their respective areas.

Broker Services

Real estate brokers are employed in the manner followed in similar commercial transactions. Under GSA procedures, brokers are also required to locate buyers and provide for wide public notice of the availability of the property. Brokers are selected from a list of available members who have informed GSA regional offices of their interest in performing broker services and who have met established standards.

Surveying

Surveying and related cadastral services are obtained by GSA from registered civil engineers or other qualified surveyors as well as land planning and development firms. Since this need is limited , GSA has not established a listing of available surveyors. Regional Offices usually employ local surveyors under a selective professional services contract. Surveyors should inform the appropriate GSA regional office of their availability and interest in the event a need develops for such work.

PUBLIC BUILDINGS SERVICE

DESIGN CONTRACTS

The Office of Design and Construction, Public Buildings Service (PBS), through its Design and Construction divisions located in the ten GSA regional offices, negotiates and administers professional services contracts with architect-engineers for the design of many new construction projects, including Federal office buildings, post offices, court houses, and research centers. Design contracts for air-conditioning systems, elevators, repairs and improvements, and extension and remodeling of existing Federal buildings are also negotiated by the GSA regional offices.

Negotiations are conducted with architect-engineers selected following an evaluations of Standard Form 251, U.S. Government Architect-Engineer Questionnaires and photos of completed projects previously filed with the GSA Regional and Central Offices by interested architect-engineers. Generally, only architect-engineers in the geographic area of the project are considered. An exception is made for projects of national significance, usually major buildings in the Washington, D.C. area, for which architect-engineers of wide reputation throughout the Nation are selected..

The architect-engineer, selected on the basis of professional competence and capability, is responsible for furnishing complete design services either from within his organization or by subcontract with consulting engineering firms which are subject to GSA approval. When a project is basically engineering in character, the prime design contract is negotiated with an engineering firm.

Topographical surveys, soil tests, and soil analyses are generally subcontracted by the architect-engineer for the particular project as reimbursable items exclusive of design fee.

The GSA regional offices also negotiate professional services contracts for the execution and installation of murals and sculptures in new Federal buildings. Artists are nominated by the architect-engineer for the building. Selection of the artist is made by GSA with the advice of recognized national, state, and/or local authorities in the field of fine arts.

CONSTRUCTION CONTRACTS

As a general rule, construction contracts for new buildings, air-conditioning, and extending or remodeling existing Federal buildings, are awarded to the lowest responsible bidder on the basis of competitive bids received after public advertising. Competitive construction bids are solicited and opened by the GSA regional office responsible for the project.

When competitive bids are solicited, a notice is placed in a newspaper in the city in which the work is to be performed. Notices also appear in various trade journals and technical publications serving the construction industry, and in the "Commerce Business Daily."

LEASING OF REAL PROPERTY

GSA leases general purpose space in urban centers in the United States, Puerto Rico, and the Virgin Islands for all Federal agencies. Outside of these urban centers, GSA leases general purpose space for all Federal agencies except for the Departments of Agriculture, Commerce, and Defense, who are permitted to do their own leasing. GSA does not lease space for Post Office purposes, nor space in foreign countries.

Leases normally are obtained by negotiation. Occasionally invitations for sealed bids are used. GSA encourages the broadest possible participation among owners and managers of acceptable commercial space.

MAINTENANCE AND REPAIR OF GOVERN-MENT-OWNED BUILDINGS

The Office of Buildings Management in the Public Buildings Service operates, maintains, repairs, and protects Government-owned and leased buildings under the control of GSA. In performing these functions it purchases a wide variety of equipment, supplies, and materials, including such items as:

Plumbing, heating, cleaning, lighting, and electrical maintenance supplies;
Carpentry, masonry, roofing, and elevator maintenance supplies;
Ventilation and air-conditioning maintenance supplies.

Buildings Operations, Maintenance and Service

cleaning
elevator operation and maintenance
electrical
painting

57

plumbing

heating

air conditioning

concessions

Mechanics' tools, hardware, and paints and painters' supplies;

Floor and window coverings, toilet supplies, and fuel and heating system supplies;

Building operating equipment, including shop equipment and fixed cafeteria equipment;

Uniforms for guards and elevator operators, including shirts, badges, and insignia; and

Office furniture and furnishings.

Many of the above items are available from the depots of the Federal Supply Service of GSA or from Federal Supply Schedule contractors, and are obtained by the Public Buildings Service from those sources.

Purchases from other than Government sources of supply are usually contracted for by authorized buildings management officials in charge of the buildings. These officials may purchase equipment, supplies, and materials not to exceed $2,500 in any single instance and may contract for janitorial, towel, window cleaning, and utility services, cafeteria operation, garbage removal, dry cleaning of uniforms, and moving (when the amount does not exceed $2,500 in each instance). If the cost involved is in excess of the limitation, the purchase is controlled by the Office of Buildings Management in the GSA regional office having jurisdiction.

Businessmen interested in selling items to the Public Buildings Service, performing buildings services, such as cleaning and window washing, or buying wastepaper, should contact their local GSA Business Service Center.

TRANSPORTATION AND COMMUNICATIONS SERVICE

The Transportation and Communications Service (TCS), on behalf of GSA, procures the Agency's transportation and

58

communications services from commercial suppliers. These services are obtained by formal advertising for bids whenever possible, or by negotiation. TCS also conducts procurements on behalf of other Federal agencies and makes contracts from which such agencies can procure as necessary. The various categories of procurements made by TCS are explained in the following paragraphs.

Additional information concerning the procurement acitivites of TCS can be obtained from GSA Business Service Centers.

COMMUNICATIONS

TCS operates the Federal Telecommunications System (FTS) for use by all Federal agencies. This system provides local and intercity telephone service and also transmits teletype, data, and other types of recorded information to various terminal devices used to send, receive, and process such information. The necessary transmission facilities are ordinarily available only from common carriers within the time allowable; therefore, TCS is often limited to placing an order with carriers for lease of such facilities. Terminal equipment, especially in the teletype, data, and other record information areas, is obtained by TCS by leasing, purchasing, or a combination thereof, with such procurement arrangements often including provision for installation and maintenance.

Other specialized communications equipment, such as radio and TV equipment, is purchased or leased through contracts with the manufacturer. Procurement and authorization for such purchase is handled through GSA, including arrangements for installation and maintenance as above stated.

Facilities and services, including the telephone instruments, required for telephone communications within a metropolitan or local area are ordered from the local telephone company by the various GSA regional offices. Such service, known as local service, can include other communications requirements. Services that are provided to distant points or are nationwide in scope are ordered and managed at the GSA Central Office level.

Upon determination by GSA (as prescribed in Federal Property Management Regulation 101-35.2) that an individual Federal agency has a communications requirement not suitable for handling on the FTS, the agency is authorized to procure the communications facility as a separate individual service.

TCS also makes areawide contracts with communication companies to provide specified service to all the agencies within certain geographic areas.

OTHER PUBLIC UTILITIES

The Office of Utilities and Communications Management of TCS, GSA Central Office, makes areawide contracts for procurement of utilities such as electricity, water, gas, and sewerage. Federal agencies in the covered geographic area then order required services individually under the contract agreement terms. Public utilities services are generally provided only by regulated utility companies or publicly owned utility companies that are non-competitive. Negotiations are conducted for acceptable rates and conditions, usually on an annual basis, although GSA has statutory authority to make contracts up to ten years in duration.

Federal agencies procure their own public utility services when area-wide contracts are not available. In the absence of GSA-negotiated rates and conditions, procurement is made in accordance with rates and schedules on file with State and Federal regulatory bodies. In general, services costing in excess of $2,500 per year are made by contract, while purchases under $2,500 per year are made by purchase order. More specific information on Federal agencies' policies for procuring public utility services can be obtained from individual agencies. (Also see Federal Property Management Regulations 101-36, and Federal Procurement Regulations 1-4.4.)

MOTOR POOLS

The Office of Motor Equipment, TCS, operates over 100 motor pools in the United States and Puerto Rico. Procurements for pool operations include motor parts and accessories, petroleum products, and the services of filling stations and repair garages. As a general rule, procurement is made through Federal Supply Service contracts negotiated by the Federal Supply Service (FSS). However, pools do make open-market purchases from local suppliers under local arrangements. Businesses supplying automotive products or services can contact any GSA Business Service Center for specific details on the best way to sell to GSA motor pools.

TCS does not contract for its own motor pool vehicles, or negotiate contracts with commercial motor vehicle rental firms. These contracting services as well as those for procuring motor vehicles for other Federal agencies are provided by FSS. Individual agencies should be contacted for information on procurement of automotive products and services for the motor vehicles they own and operate.

TRANSPORTATION

TCS, through its Office of Transportation, negotiates with transportation carriers for freight rates and services, for all GSA-controlled shipments, and, on behalf of civil agencies, for freight rates and services on shipment of property over 100 short tons, and smaller shipments which in the aggregate are over 100 short tons. Negotiations are conducted with individual carriers, carriers' conferences, committees, or associations. TCS also negotiates with the carrier industry, at an agency's request, to effect a contract for special transportation service. In this connection, see Federal property Management Regulations 101–40, and Federal Procurement Regulations 1–19.

TCS contracts with, among others, drayage firms for metropolitan area drayage where tonnage is large; with ocean freight forwarders; and with firms for packing, crating, and marking. Bids for these transportation services are requested through formal advertising, or in some cases through informal negotiation.

Information relating to transportation procurements effected by TCS can be obtained from any GSA regional office. Information relating to agency procurement of transportation services in connection with their shipments of under 100 short tons should be obtained from the individual agencies.

FEDERAL SUPPLY SERVICE

Most Federal agencies have their own purchasing activity and buy the predominant volume of items peculiar to their own needs. In general, the Federal Supply Service (FSS) of GSA is responsible for supplying items common to the needs of Federal agencies, and is a steady market for thousands of common-use items, some of which are categorized below:

OFFICE SUPPLIES AND EQUIPMENT
HOUSEHOLD AND OFFICE FURNITURE
HAND TOOLS
REFRIGERATORS, AIR-CONDITIONERS, AND WATER COOLERS
AUTOMOTIVE VEHICLES AND OTHER MOTOR-PROPELLED VEHICLES
PAINT
EDP MAGNETIC TAPE
TYPEWRITERS AND OTHER OFFICE MACHINES
ENVELOPES AND STATIONERY
MAINTENANCE AND OPERATING SUPPLIES AND EQUIPMENT such as: Laundry equipment, coolers and dispensers, safety equipment, plumbing and heating fixtures and accessories, hand and machine tools, bolts, studs, nuts, washers, nails, fuses, switches, connectors, and other electrical supplies, medical equipment and supplies, floor covering, paints, waxes, adhesives, household furnishings, hand pumps, filters, pipe, and tubing.
FIREFIGHTING EQUIPMENT such as: Ropes, pumps, hose, hand tools, medical kits, mess outfits, compasses, surgical dressings and material, saddlery, axes, lanterns, blankets, sleeping bags, and tents.
ADMINISTRATIVE SUPPLIES such as: Printing, duplicat-

ing, and photographic equipment and supplies, fastening devices, sound recording equipment, packing and packaging materials, drafting and surveying instruments, twine, scales, brushes, and brief cases.

FSS PROCUREMENT IS DIVIDED INTO 5 MAJOR PROGRAMS

SUPPLY DEPOTS

Under this program approximately 50,000 common items are bought under various types of contracts and stocked in supply depots. GSA's supply depots are located so as to service economically and efficiently the requirements of Government agencies in all geographical areas of the United States and overseas.

Agencies submit their requisitions to the appropriate GSA regional office and their orders are filled from stock, unless the order is so large that direct delivery from the supplier is more advantageous.

Most contracting for supply depot items is accomplished under centralized procurement programs by the FSS, GSA Central Office. However, contracts for some items are executed by individual GSA regional offices, which are national in scope and are utilized by other regions requiring such items for depot stocks.

FEDERAL SUPPLY SCHEDULES

When the volume of orders for a particular item is too large or too small to warrant handling on a storage and issue basis, and under certain other conditions, the item may be purchased under indefinite quantity term contracts commonly known as Federal Supply Schedules. Federal Supply Schedules are usually issued every year and cover more than 700,000 items such as automotive parts and accessories, tires, batteries, furniture, electric lamps (bulbs), paper products, photographic and duplicating supplies, and athletic equipment.

In most cases, schedule contracts are executed by the FSS at its Central Office. Federal Supply Schedule contracts for some commodities, however, are entered into by GSA regional offices. Using agencies submit their purchase orders direct to the supplier, and delivery is made direct to the using agency or point of use.

Advertisements for bids on new Federal Supply Schedule contracts take place prior to the end of the contract period (one year or less). No specific quantity can be stated in the invitation for bids; however, sales figures are shown for the most recent period possible. Under certain conditions contracts are negotiated.

CONSOLIDATED PURCHASE CONTRACTS

Certain items which have a substantial recurring demand are sometimes not suitable for inclusion in either the depot or Federal Supply Schedule programs. Agency requirements for those items are consolidated by GSA and special definite quantity contracts executed, for direct delivery to the using agency or point of use. These contracts are usually advertised under formal procurement procedures but in some cases may be negotiated.

DIRECT ORDER PURCHASING

GSA provides, upon request, special procurement service to agencies which lack technical personnel or experience in purchasing certain items, or which believe that GSA can buy more advantageously because of its knowledge of the market. GSA also makes purchases for direct delivery to using agencies under special agreements. For example, GSA buys the foreign aid program requirements of the Agency for International Development.

Many direct procurements are also caused by exceptions to regulations, or by special conditions. For example, an abnormally large quantity of a Federal Supply Schedule item might exceed the maximum order limitation of the Schedule, thus creating a need for a special purchase.

AUTOMATIC DATA PROCESSING PROCUREMENT PROGRAM

Automatic Data Processing (ADP) is a billion dollar business in the Federal Government. It is also one of the fastest growing of the Government's business interests. The Federal Government is the largest single user of ADP equipment in the Nation. Currently, 48 departments and agencies operate 3,908 computers in 3,076 ADP units located in 237 cities throughout the country.

In recognition of ADP's national importance and impact on Government affairs, Congress passed an amendment to the Property Act which provides for the central operational management (including procurement) of all ADP Government matters in GSA. The Office of Automated Data Management Services, FSS is responsible for administering this amendment to the Property Act, and as such, is the central coordination control point for all Federal Government ADP procurement requirements. This procurement program is dedicated to the single purchaser concept and contracting delegations are only authorized when it is to the best interest of the Government to do so.

GSA's interest in this area encompasses the full range of Government ADP logistical requirements including contracting for: major computer systems, (hardware); technical development (software); services (data acquisition, conversion, computer time); support commodities (communications, peripheral equipment); supplies (cards, forms, magnetic tape); replacement (obsolete and excess equipment); and leasing of ADP equipment.

NEW OR IMPROVED ITEMS OF SUPPLY

General Services Administration has established specific procedures to assist businessmen in presenting new or improved supply items or services. Those procedures provide that the prospective supplier submit inquiries to the nearest GSA Business Service Center, describing the item in detail and listing other pertinent information.

Upon receipt of the inquiry, a determination is made at the regional level as to whether the item is similar to any item currently purchased by GSA. If the item is similar, the prospective supplier is furnished the appropriate bidders' mailing list application forms and the necessary instructions to permit submission of bids on future contracts for the item.

If the item is not similar, the prospective supplier is requested to prepare GSA Form 1171, Application for Presenting New or Improved Articles.

This application must be submitted in triplicate to the nearest Business Service Center, together with any descriptive literature, drawings, plans, price lists, and similar supporting data. However, in instances where the nature and usage of the item presented is such that procurement by GSA is not likely, the Business Service Center will advise the businessman and provide appropriate counseling with respect to other agencies' procurement potential.

Upon receipt of the completed GSA Form 1171 by the Business Service Center, the form is sent to the Procurement Operations Division, Federal Supply Service, Washington, D.C. 20406. That office makes an evaluation of the merits and usefulness of the item and determines its acceptability. The Business Service Center and the applicant are notified of final action on the application. When warranted, tests may be conducted normally at the expense of the prospective supplier, to

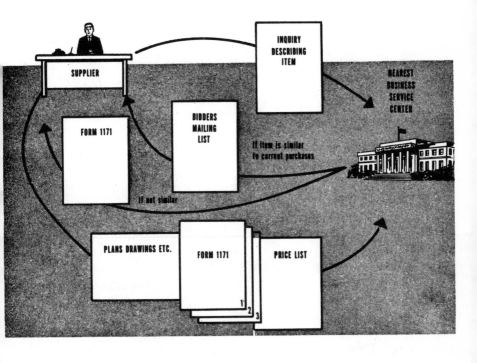

verify that the product will measure up to the performance claimed.

The GSA Central Office initiates the necessary action to add approved items to the proper Federal Supply Schedule or to GSA depot stocks. The Central Office also estimates the quantity that may be required for Government use.

If it is determined not to buy the article, the prospective supplier is promptly notified by letter, which will include the reasons for rejection. It should be understood that before an item can be approved for inclusion in the Federal supply system, it must have an indicated demand sufficient to warrant the cost and effort of establishing a Federal Supply Schedule or placing it in depot inventory on a nationwide basis.

The fact that an item is rejected by GSA does not prevent a manufacturer from contacting individual Federal agencies for the purpose of selling his products. If a sufficient number of individual agencies buy the product through direct contacts, a demand may develop which would justify inclusion of the item in GSA's Government-wide supply system.

REGULAR ITEMS OF SUPPLY

Businessmen wishing to participate in competitive bidding on regular items of supply should be guided by the following procedures:

1. The supplier should contact the nearest GSA Regional Office, directing his inquiry to the Regional Director of Business Affairs. In reply, the supplier will receive a copy of:
   A. Standard Form 129—Bidder's Mailing List Application.
   B. GSA Form 1382—List of Commodities.
   C. GSA Form 1783—Bidder's Mailing List Services Code Sheet.
   D. GSA Form 1754—Bidder's Mailing List Application Code Sheet.
   E. GSA Form 2459—Bidder's Mailing List Instructions.

2. Under this procedure, it is not necessary to submit additional forms to any other GSA office.

ADVICE TO PROSPECTIVE SUPPLIERS

PROSPECTIVE SUPPLIERS SHOULD . . .

CONTACT the nearest GSA Business Service Center for information about where to offer products and services and where to get publications and other aids to Government purchasing.

CONSULT the daily published lists showing what the Government is buying—daily GSA bid postings and the "Commerce Business Daily."

KNOW what GSA is buying by obtaining copies of the GSA *Stock Catalog* and Federal specification.

GET ON GSA's bidders' mailing lists—submit applications for mailing lists on the basis of individual items rather than by categories of items—and completely describe the item on which bids are submitted, preferably in specification language.

BE CERTAIN before submitting bids that the dates of the specifications used in determining price, responsiveness, and the probable acceptability of products agree with the dates of the specifications cited in the invitation for bids.

USE the utmost care in stating the accuracy of a product's performance, price, and other pertinent factors.

PROTECT retention on bidders' mailing lists by either submitting bids or by notifying the purchasing activity of continued interest.

VERIFY all entries on bids and check adherence to bid specifications in order that bids will be acceptable—know exactly what is expected before bidding on the proposed Government contract.

PREPARE and mail bids or offers in time for receipt prior to the established deadline specified in the solicitation. A rejected late bid or offer may be avoided if the offeror is aware of the guidance provided in FPR 1–2.303 and follows the specific instructions contained in the solicitation.

GSA Enhances Sales Opportunities By—

1. Limiting many orders for small business competition only.
2. Accepting bids for partial quantities.
3. Allowing adequate bidding time.
4. Establishing reasonable delivery schedules.
5. Using recognized industry standards.

PART 4
Other civil agencies with major supply activities

CIVIL AGENCY PROCUREMENT PROCEDURES

Purchasing by civil agencies of the Federal Government is nationwide in scope, but is generally decentralized to permit regional and field offices to buy the bulk of their own requirements.

In virtually all cases the purchasing authority delegated by agencies to field offices is adequate to cover normal operating needs. Clearance with higher levels of authority is required only in exceptional cases. These exceptions usually involve high-dollar value purchases; but central office approval may also be necessary for some negotiated procurements or for purchases of technical products and services. In some instances, the headquarters office may consolidate field office requirements for centralized procurement, in the interest of economy or because of other other considerations.

73

HOW AGENCIES CONTACT SOURCES OF SUPPLY

There is no uniform procedure by which business concerns can bring their products to the attention of all Federal agencies. Most agencies rely upon business firms to demonstrate an interest in Government supply contracts by submitting completed Standard Form 129, Bidder's Mailing List Application, either to the central or field offices of the agency.

When any of the items listed by the supplier on his application are being considered for purchase, a copy of the bid invitation will be sent to him. In many instances, manufacturers and original suppliers reserve the right to sell to the Government direct. Therefore, dealers and agents should bid only within their franchised contracts.

When quotations are requested for export and it is stated in the invitation for bids that sales and service representation in the designated country is required, failure to meet the requirement will result in rejection of the bid. When the invitation calls for complete material, drawings, or other details which thoroughly describe the items on which the bid is submitted, these must be furnished or the bid may be rejected. These data are necessary in order to make adequate evaluation of the quotations received.

In order to obtain the maximum number of bids, agencies attempt to give as much publicity as possible to proposed procurements. One or more of the following methods are used by Federal agencies in contacting possible sources of supply:

1. Distribution of invitations for bids to comprehensive mailings lists of known suppliers.
2. Use of mailing lists secured from trade journals and directories.
3. Publicizing proposed procurements of $10,000 or more in the "Commerce Business Daily."
4. Furnishing copies of current bid invitations to commercial agencies that publish the information for use by their subscribers.

5. Public posting of invitations for bids.
6. Paid advertising in newspapers, trade journals, and other media.
7. Providing news releases about major procurements to newspapers, wire services, radio and television stations, and other communications media.
8. Encouraging industry sales representatives to keep Government contracting officers informed of new or improved products.

Standard Form 129 and other standard forms commonly used in Government procurement are illustrated in the Appendix. Copies of these forms are available without charge from any Government procurement office or GSA Business Service Center.

BIDDERS' MAILING LISTS

Normally, the submission of Standard Form 129—with complete and exact information about the products on which the supplier wishes to bid—is sufficient to secure placement on an agency's mailings list. Often, however, the agency will require additional information for assurance that the prospective supplier is capable of satisfactory performance under a specific contract. Agencies may request that information of the following nature be submitted along with Standard Form 129:
1. Production capability for the items involved.
2. A description of the products normally produced by the prospective supplier.
3. Number of present employees.
4. Available plant and transportation facilities.
5. Previous experience with Government contracts.
6. Financial status and other pertinent facts to indicate the responsible character of the firm.
7. Related information which indicates the nature and scope of the firm's operations.

An evaluation of this information by the agency prior to placing a firm on a bidder's mailing list results in the saving of considerable time and money by both the agency and the prospective supplier.

Company catalogs should not be submitted to Federal agencies with a request that the company be placed on the mailing list for all items listed in the catalog. This type of blanket request requires too great a workload for the average Government purchasing department to handle.

It should be understood that submission of Standard Form 129 results only in the prospective bidder being placed on the mailing list of the agency to which the form was submitted. No central agency in the Government places the names of bidders on all Government mailing lists.

CIVIL AGENCY PROCUREMENT PROGRAMS

The supply needs of many of the smaller Federal agencies are limited almost entirely to administrative items, such as office supplies, bought primarily from GSA. Because many requests to sell these items to an agency would normally be referred to GSA, considerable time could be saved by contacting the nearest GSA Business Service Center. The general classes of products procured by GSA are described in Part II of this publication.

The following pages describe the general procurement programs of those agencies with major supply activities and substantial open-market purchases.

ATOMIC ENERGY COMMISSION

Atomic Energy Commission procurement does not follow the usual Government supply pattern. The bulk of the procurement of supplies and services in connection with AEC programs is done by the contractors which operate AEC plants and laboratories. These include plants for the production of uranium feed materials, special nuclear materials, and atomic weapons;

nuclear reactors; and research laboratories. Most of the purchasing of material, equipment and supplies required for the program is done in the field by these AEC contractors.

The questions of "What does AEC buy," and "Where to quote on AEC requirements," are best answered by reference to AEC's own publications. A pamphlet entitled "Selling to AEC," which lists the products the Agency purchases and includes a directory of its purchasing offices and contractors, is available from the Superintendent of Documents, U.S. Government Printing Office, Washington, D.C. 20402. A pamphlet entitled "Contracting for Construction and Related Architect-Engineering Services," which discusses policies, methods of operation, and types of contracts involved in construction of AEC-owned facilities, is available from the same source.

Businessmen interested in selling to AEC should procure these pamphlets since they provide information on AEC's procurement activities.

DEPARTMENT OF AGRICULTURE

The purchasing activities and requirements of the Department of Agriculture are varied because of the many types of programs for which this Agency is responsible.

In soil and forest conservation work, the Department buys earth-moving and other heavy equipment, such as tractors, graders, compressors, concrete mixers, and cranes; construction materials; petroleum products; expolsives; radio equipment; surveying equipment; and a wide selection of tools and hardware supplies.

In marketing, research, and stabilization services, it buys laboratory and testing equipment, such as spectrophotometers, microscopes, scales and balances, moisture meters, and precision sieves; special types of trays, boxes and bags; all types of farm and shop equipment; photographic supplies and equipment; and maintenance equipment for laboratory work shops, greenhouses, insectaries, and other activities.

In other programs, the Department buys electronic equipment

for testing and developmental purposes, books, library supplies, industry and market surveys, exhibit design and construction, services for both motion and still picture production work, and a large variety of other supplies and services.

The Department's Office of Plant and Operations exercises general responsibility for all phases of the Department's procurement, supply and property management functions and for the acquisition, management, utilization, and disposition of Department owned and leased real estate.

The Department has prepared its own pamphlet, entitled "Selling to U.S.D.A.," which is available without charge from the Contract and Procurement Management Division, Office of Plant and Operations, U.S. Department of Agriculture, Washington, D.C. 20250. This pamphlet provides general information about Agriculture's procurement procedures. It describes how and where the requirements of each agency of the Department are procured. It also includes a current directory of Department of Agriculture purchasing offices and their locations.

DEPARTMENT OF COMMERCE

This Department provides a centralized procurement service for administrative type purchases (supplies, equipment, materials and services) for practically all of the organizational elements of the Department. Inquiries relative to these procurements, bidders' lists, procurement policies, or assistance and guidance should be directed to the Office of Administrative Services Procurement Division, U.S. Department of Commerce, Washington, D.C. 20230.

Specialized procurement needs of the Maritime Administration and the National Bureau of Standards, and to a lesser extent of the Environmental Science Services Administration and the Bureau of the Census, are handled on a decentralized basis. Inquiries on such specialized procurement needs as well as the submission of bidder's mailing list applications should be directed to the following locations:

Maritime Administration
Office of Property and Supply
Division of Purchases and Sales
Washington, D.C. 20235

National Bureau of Standards
Supply Division
Procurement Section
Washington, D.C. 20234

Bureau of the Census
Procurement and Supply Management Branch
Federal Office Building #4
Suitland, Maryland 20233

Environmental Science Services Administration
Administrative Operations Division
Procurement Management Section
Rockville, Maryland 20852

The Department can also provide a pamphlet, at no charge, which provides general information about the Department's procurement procedures. This pamphlet, entitled "How to Sell to the U.S. Department of Commerce," also contains a directory of the Commerce Field Offices which can provide valuable assistance to business firms.

DEPARTMENT OF HEALTH, EDUCATION, AND WELFARE

This Department procures a wide variety of articles and services for staff and operational programs involving health, education, and social security general welfare fields. The greatest dollar volume of buys for such operational program requirements are made by procuring activities of the Public Health Service.

Since procurement responsibility is decentralized, business-men may wish to direct inquiries to the Departmental Regional Office located nearest them. These offices are located in Boston, Massachusetts; New York, New York; Charlottesville, Virginia; Atlanta, Georgia; Chicago, Illinois; Kansas City, Missouri; Dallas, Texas; Denver, Colorado; and San Francisco, California. Inquiries regarding overall Departmental procurements should be addressed to the Director, Division of Procurement and Supply Management, OASA-OGS, Department of Health, Education, and Welfare, Washington, D.C. 20201.

For headquarters offices in downtown Washington, D.C., the preponderance of administrative articles and services not acquired from other Federal agencies are bought by the Procurement Section, Executive Office, Office of the Secretary, Department of Health, Education, and Welfare, Washington, D.C. 20201.

DEPARTMENT OF THE INTERIOR

Since the Department of the Interior has placed procurement responsibility in each of its various bureaus, there is very little open-market purchasing by the Office of the Secretary. Businessmen interested in presenting new, improved, or regular items of supply for the attention of the central headquarters office usually do so through personal visits; by mail; or by demonstrations arranged through contact with the Division of Property and Records. Bureaus under the Department of the Interior include: Bureau of Commercial Fisheries, Bureau of Sport Fisheries and Wildlife, National Park Service, Bureau of Mines, Geological Survey, Bureau of Indian Affairs, Bureau of Land Management, Federal Water Pollution Control Administration, Bureau of Reclamation, Bonneville Power Administration, Southwestern Power Administration and Alaska Power Administration.

NATIONAL PARK SERVICE

Approximately 80 percent of this Agency's supplies are procured through the facilities of GSA. Contracts for most physical improvements are let to general contractors to furnish all labor, material and supplies. Concession contracts are let for concessionaires to furnish accommodations and services for park visitors. Concessionaires are free to select their own sources of supply. A list of concession contractors may be obtained by addressing an inquiry to the Chief of Concessions Management, National Park Service, Department of the Interior, Washington, D.C. 20240.

The bulk of the National Park Service purchasing has been decentralized to its field offices. A list of the offices issuing invitations to bid may be obtained from the Chief of Property Management, National Park Service, Department of the Interior, Washington, D.C. 20240.

GEOLOGICAL SURVEY

Geological Survey purchases many kinds of special supplies and furniture, including instruments and equipment for drafting, surveying, and chemical laboratory work; electronic equipment; special chemicals, sensitized film, and other photographic supplies; office equipment; metals; lumber; machine parts; and hand tools.

Contracts are entered into for helicopter flying time, aerial photography, and test hole and core drilling. Businessmen should write or visit the Branch of Contracts, U.S Geological Survey, Department of the Interior, Washington, D.C. 20240.

BUREAU OF COMMERCIAL FISHERIES

This Bureau buys small boats, fishing nets and other gear, laboratory and scientific equipment, and other items related to commercial fishing. Inquiries should be directed to the Branch of

Property Management, Bureau of Commercial Fisheries, 1801 North Moore Street, Arlington, Virginia 22209, or to any one of the Bureau's seven regional and area offices.

BUREAU OF MINES

The Bureau's procurement is primarily decentralized throughout its field research centers, laboratories, area and district offices, and helium activity. These installations are engaged in research relating to the conservation and development of mineral resources; helium conservation, production, and supply; promotion of health and safety in mines and in the mineral industries; and controlling fires in coal deposits. A large part of the Bureau's purchases are for laboratory supplies and equipment and helium production equipment and materials.

Prospective suppliers may file Standard Form 129, Bidders Mailing List Application, with any Bureau field office. A list of offices issuing invitations to bid may be obtained from the Chief, Division of Procurement and Property Management, Bureau of Mines, Department of the Interior, Washington, D.C. 20240.

BUREAU OF SPORT FISHERIES AND WILDLIFE

This Bureau buys small boats, outboard motors, construction and farming equipment, two-way radio transmitters and receivers, and fish foods. Business representatives should send inquiries to the Procurement Officer, Bureau of Sport Fisheries and Wildlife, Department of the Interior, Washington, D.C. 20240, or to any one of its six regional offices.

BUREAU OF INDIAN AFFAIRS

The supply requirements of this Bureau consist of agricultural materials, building and maintenance supplies and equipment, road and irrigation construction equipment and supplies, subsistence items, and miscellaneous school supplies. Since purchasing and contracting authority is vested in the area directors of the Bureau, all inquries or requests to be placed on mailing lists should be directed to the nearest area office. The names and addresses of those offices are listed in the "Purchasing and Sales Directory," published by the Small Business Administration.

BUREAU OF RECLAMATION

Decentralized purchasing within the Bureau is conducted through regional and project offices located in the 17 western states. With the exception of specially designed equipment, purchases are generally made by offices in or near the area in which delivery is required. The Office of the Chief Engineer in Denver, Colorado, is the central purchasing office for large items of electrical and mechanical equipment requiring engineering design and drawing data, such as generators, turbines, transformers, and circuit breakers. Suppliers desiring to participate in Bureau purchases should direct their requests to the office in the area which they normally serve. If the supplier wants to quote on the requirements of several offices, a request should be sent to each office concerned. Requests should be limited to supplies which are usually bought through local distributors and which are readily available through existing distribution channels. Inquiries about more specialized equipment should be directed to the Chief Engineer, Bureau of Reclamation, Department of the Interior, Building 67, Denver Federal Center, Denver, Colorado 80225.

BUREAU OF LAND MANAGEMENT

Purchasing within the Bureau is decentralized and is conducted through Service Centers and State Offices in ten western states and Alaska, -as well as in Washington, D.C. These Offices

83

purchase firefighting equipment, radio and communications equipment, surveying instruments, range grass seed, brushland plows, rangeland drills, and heavy equipment. They also contract for construction of earthfill dams, fences, roads and for land treatment work such as plowing, seeding, and aerial spraying. Purchases exceeding the open market limitation of $2,500 ($2,000 for construction) are handled by formal bid invitations. For information on procurement activities of the Bureau, contact the nearest Service Center or the Washington office, as listed in the "Purchasing and Sales Directory," published by the Small Business Administration.

ALASKA POWER ADMINISTRATION

Alaska Power Administration maintains procurement activities at its headquarters in Juneau, Alaska, and at the Eklutna Project hydro-electric powerplant (located near Anchorage, Alaska). Purchases are generally limited to those applicable to the operation and maintenance of a hydroelectric powerplant. General supplies are procured through the facilities of GSA. Inquiries should be directed to the Alaska Power Administration, P.O. Box 50, Juneau, Alaska 99801.

BONNEVILLE POWER ADMINISTRATION

Bonneville Power Administration purchases materials which, in general, are utilized in 115,000, 230,000, and 345,000 and higher voltage lines and substations. Purchases are mostly of a specialized nature and generally are purchased from large manufacturers. All purchases are made from the Procurement Office, Bonneville Power Administration, Department of the Interior, Portland, Oregon 97208.

SOUTHWESTERN POWER ADMINISTRATION

Southwestern Power Administration maintains a centralized procurement activity at Tulsa, Oklahoma. Inquiries should be sent to the Southwestern Power Administration, U.S. Post Office and Federal Office Building, 333 West 4th Street, Tulsa, Oklahoma 74101. Commodities purchased are generally limited to those applicable to construction, operation, and maintenance of high voltage transmission systems.

FEDERAL WATER POLLUTION CONTROL ADMINISTRATION

All items exceeding $2,500 in cost are purchased by the Washington office of FWPCA. Purchases less than $2,500 are made by individual offices and laboratories located nationwide. The major portion of purchases are chemicals, supplies and equipment; small boats, motors and water sampling devices. Businessmen should write or visit the Procurement Branch, Federal Water Pollution Control Administration, U.S. Department of the Interior, 1921 Jefferson Davis Highway, Crystal Mall, Arlington, Virgina 22209.

DEPARTMENT OF JUSTICE

The various Bureaus and Services under this Department are responsible for their own procurement, with the Department itself only buying to cover its own needs. Requirements of the various Bureaus include paper and paper products, fingerprint supplies, arms and ammunition, handcuffs and leg irons, medical supplies and equipment, and miscellaneous office supplies and equipment.

BUREAU OF PRISONS

Prisons procure practically all general types of commodities since many of them are in effect self-contained cities. Purchases of end products are made by the individual prisons from local sources of supply or from national supply houses.

Inquiries or applications for inclusion on mailing lists should be directed to specific penal institutions. Personal contacts by company representatives are recommended, but should be arranged sufficiently in advance to permit appropriate technicians and interested officials to be present, particularly for demonstrations of new or improved products. Businessmen making general inquiry about doing business with the Federal prison system should visit or write to the Bureau of Prisons, Department of Justice, Washington, D.C. 20537.

FEDERAL PRISON INDUSTRIES

This corporation purchases the raw materials required in the various work shops, usually under negotiated contracts. Materials purchased include steel, for steel furniture construction; wool and cotton, for wool and cotton mill production; textile fabrics, for production of clothing; leather, for shoe production; bristles, for the production of brushes; lumber, for the production of wood furniture; and broom corn, for the production of brooms. Federal prison products are for sale to Government agencies only, usually through the facilities of GSA. Inquiries and requests to be put on mailing lists for raw materials should be directed to the Purchasing Division, Federal Prison Industries, Inc., Department of Justice, Washington, D.C. 20537.

FEDERAL BUREAU OF INVESTIGATION

The major commodities purchased by this Bureau are radio and electronic equipment and special laboratory equipment. The FBI also purchases guns, ammunition, and other types of law enforcement supplies and equipment. Inquiries with regard to FBI procurement, or visits of business representatives who are interested in selling their products, should be made to the Property Management Unit, Federal Bureau of Investigation, Department of Justice, Washington, D.C. 20535.

BUREAU OF NARCOTICS AND DANGEROUS DRUGS

The procurement interest of this Bureau centers primarily in communications equipment, laboratory equipment, guns, ammunition and other types of law enforcement equipment and supplies. Inquiries with regard to BNDD procurement should be made to the Bureau of Narcotics and Dangerous Drugs, Administrative Services Division, Washington, D.C. 20537.

DEPARTMENT OF THE TREASURY

With the exception of the Bureau of the Mint, the Bureau of Engraving and Printing, and the Internal Revenue Service, relatively few invitations for bid are issued by the Department of the Treasury.

The Bureau of the Mint purchases items such as melting furnaces, rolling mills, heat-treating furnaces, blanking presses, and stamping presses. Inquiries with regard to such purchases should be sent to the Superintendent, United States Mint, Philadelphia, Pennsylvania 19130 or Superintendent, United States Mint, Denver, Colorado 80204.

Among the specialized items procured by the Bureau of Engraving and Printing are papers used for currency and bonds, special formula inks and dye colors and various pieces of custom manufactured production equipment. Inquiries to the Bureau of Engraving and Printing should be sent to the Director, Bureau of Engraving and Printing, Department of the Treasury, Washington, D.C. 20226.

The Internal Revenue Service purchases miscellaneous ADP equipment and supplies and special mail handling equipment. Inquiries should be sent to Chief, Contract and Procurement Section, Internal Revenue Service, Washington, D.C. 20224.

DEPARTMENT OF TRANSPORTATION

Procurement is decentralized throughout the Department of Transportation with each of the operating administrations procuring their own requirements. Procurement by the Office of the Secretary of Transportation primarily involves contracting with management consultant firms for the development of studies covering a variety of programs within the spheres of responsibility of the Department. Information concerning doing business with the Office of the Secretary may be obtained by contacting the Procurement Division, Office of Administrative Operations, Washington, D.C. 20590.

FEDERAL AVIATION ADMINISTRATION

The Federal Aviation Administration purchases a wide variety of equipment, supplies and supporting spare parts in the aircraft, communications, air navigation, and air traffic control fields. These procurements are made at various locations throughout the country, depending upon the type of requirements to be satisfied. Some procurements are made at headquarters in Washington, D.C. These are primarily concerned with research and development and with the acquisition of major air navigational and air traffic control systems for worldwide installations; some at the Aeronautical Center at Oklahoma City; still others are made at each of the FAA regions within the United States. Further information concerning Federal Aviation Administration procurements may be obtained by contacting the Procurement Information Office, Procurement Operations Division, Federal Aviation Administration, Washington, D.C. 20553, or any FAA regional office.

FEDERAL HIGHWAY ADMINISTRATION

The Federal Highway Administration purchases all types of road construction equipment, automotive vehicles and repairs parts, maintenance support equipment and related materials and supplies. The majority of these items are for use on highway development programs in foreign countries and are procured by the Washington procurement office, which also purchases research and development services as required for such purposes as improvement in vehicular safety standards; testing of vehicles; and development of electronically controlled access to highway approaches. Business concerns desiring to do business with this Administration should submit Standard Form 129, Bidder's Mailing List Application, to the Federal Highway Administration, Procurement Branch, 1717 H Street NW., Washington, D.C. 20591.

U.S. COAST GUARD

Procurement in the U.S. Coast Guard is decentralized; however, in its Washington, D.C. office procurement is effected for vessels, aircraft, electronics equipment, outfitting equipment and supplies for new vessels, research services and other material to support Coast Guard operations. As the Coast Guard is basically of a military character, the contracts of the Department of the Navy and the other military services are used when practical to procure its requirements. Inquiries pertaining to doing business with the U.S. Coast Guard should be directed to Commandant (FS-1), U.S. Coast Guard, 1300 E Street NW., Washington, D.C. 20591.

FEDERAL RAILROAD ADMINISTRATION

This Administration contracts for research and development in high speed ground transportation, including but not limited to, aerodynamics, vehicle propulsion, vehicle control, communications and guideways. The Administration's procurement office is located in Room 211, Donohoe Building, 400–6 Street S.W., Washington, D.C. 20591. The Alaska Railroad purchases all of its requirements for the maintenance and operation of the railroad. Firms desiring to sell to the roalroad may contact the Procurement Officer, Alaska Railroad, P.O. Box 7-2111, Anchorage, Alaska.

URBAN MASS TRANSPORTATION ADMINISTRATION

Research contracts constitute the principal procurement activity of the Urban Mass Transportation Administration. Information on procurement may be obtained directly from UMTA, Washington, D.C. 20591.

ST. LAWRENCE SEAWAY DEVELOPMENT CORPORATION

The St. Lawrence Seaway Development Corporation procures a wide variety of navigational lock operating equipment and related maintenance parts; also heavy construction equipment and repair parts. Information on procurement may be obtained from St. Lawrence Seaway Development Corporation, Administrative Services Officer, P.O. Box 520, Massena, New York 13662.

NATIONAL AERONAUTICS AND SPACE ADMINISTRATION

The Act which established the National Aeronautics and Space Administration requires that the statutory rules governing procurement by the military services be followed by NASA. As a result, the policies and procedures set forth in the NASA Procurement Regulation (NPC–400) are generally similar to the Armed Services Procurement Regulation.

The NASA procurement system is decentralized. Each of NASA's field installations makes its own contracts for support of its operations, for equipment, for construction, and for research and development projects assigned to the installation.

The supplies and services which these installations buy are in the thousands—from routine office supplies (primarily from GSA) to complex construction projects, from nuts and bolts and miniature electronic components to large spacecraft systems. Also included are complex instrumentation and controls necessary for operation of test centers.

More details about NASA procurement and organization are contained in the publication, "Selling to NASA," available without charge from national headquarters (Washington, D.C. 20546) or any of the following centers: Ames Research Center, Moffett Field, California 94035; Electronics Research Center, 575 Technology Square, Cambridge, Massachusetts 02139; Flight Research Center, P.O. Box 273, Edwards, California 93523; Goddard Space Flight Center, Greenbelt, Maryland 20771; Jet Propulsion Laboratory, 4800 Oak Grove Drive, Pasadena, California 91103; John F. Kennedy Space Center, Florida 32899; Langley Research Center, Langley Station, Hampton, Virginia 23365; Lewis Research Center, 21000 Brookpark Road, Cleveland, Ohio 44135; Manned Spacecraft Center, Houston, Texas 77058; Marshall Space Flight Center, Alabama 35812; NASA Pasadena Office, 4800 Oak Grove Drive, Pasadena, California 91103; Wallops Station, Wallops Island, Virginia 23337.

POST OFFICE DEPARTMENT

Post Office Department procurement involves a variety of equipment peculiar to its own needs such as postage meters, stamp vending machines, canceling machines, letterboxes, letter sorting machines, and installed mechanization including parcel sorters, sack sorters, bulk conveyor systems and monorail systems. Also, equipment designed for special needs such as scales, portable conveyors, and workroom furniture including cases and tables (fabricated out of both wood and steel). In addition to equipment, the Department buys special types of inks, steel shelving, safes, stools, baskets, lockers, cabinets, pouch and bag racks, and stamp boxes.

Inquiries regarding bidders' mailing lists or the Department's interest in specific items of supply should be forwarded to the Director, Procurement Division, Bureau of Facilities, U.S. Post Office Department, Washington, D.C. 20260. In Washington, personal visits may be made to Room 7407, Post Office Department, 12th and Pennsylvania Avenue NW. POD regional

91

offices also procure a variety of non-standard equipment and services, particularly automotive vehicle truck and trailer rental, custodial services, building and equipment maintenance services, and vehicle maintenance. Information concerning field procurements can be obtained from the Chief, Procurement and Supply Branch of the Post Office Department regional offices located in the following cities: Atlanta, Georgia; Boston, Massachusetts; Chicago, Illinois; Cincinnati, Ohio; Dallas, Texas; Denver, Colorado; Memphis, Tennessee; Minneapolis, Minnesota; New York, New York; Philadelphia, Pennsylvania; St. Louis, Missouri; San Francisco, California; Seattle, Washington; Washington, D.C.; and Wichita, Kansas.

Repair parts for electrical, electronic and mechanical equipment and assemblies are procured by the Repair Parts Facility located at the Western Area Supply Center, Topeka, Kansas 66601. Inquiries regarding bidders' mailing lists for the supply of repair parts should be directed to the foregoing facility.

TENNESSEE VALLEY AUTHORITY

Tennessee Valley Authority purchases are primarily for construction and operation of electric power plants and transmission systems, construction of dams and locks, and development and experimental production of fertilizers.

Purchases include turbogenerators, steam generating units, nuclear plant equipment, hydraulic turbines and generators, transformers, boilers, piping systems, and switchgear; coal, coke, and nuclear fuel; electrical and electronic supplies, equipment, and spare parts; communication equipment and supplies, including structural and milled steel; phosphate rock and chemicals; and medical, laboratory, and photographic equipment and supplies.

TVA purchases are centralized in its Division of Purchasing in Chattanooga, Tennessee. Each purchasing agent in this Division specializes in buying certain commodities and maintains mailing lists of suppliers for the commodities he controls. Businessmen should get on the mailing lists for the products on which they desire to bid, and should keep the purchasing agents informed about new or improved products.

Requests for information or for mailing list applications on all products (except coal, coke, and nuclear fuel) should be addressed to: Chief, General Procurement Branch, Division of Purchasing, Tennessee Valley Authority, Chattanooga, Tennessee 37401. Inquiries about coal, coke, and nuclear fuel should be directed to: Chief, Fuels Procurement Branch, at the same location. Inquiries about transportation services should be directed to: Chief, Traffic Branch, at the same location.

VETERANS ADMINISTRATION

The Veterans Administration operates a nationwide system of 245 hospitals, nursing home care units and domiciliaries, each of which is a self-sustaining unit. In addition to the medical requirements commonly associated with hospital operations, these facilities operate power plants, restaurants, fire and protective services, laundries, garages, warehouses, apartments, recreation areas, television and motion picture entertainment systems, and pharmacies. These units require all types of equipment, supplies and services that such operations entail. In addition, the VA has been assigned Government-wide procurement and distribution responsibility for civilian agency requirements for subsistence and drugs.

VA regional offices and data processing centers buy mostly administrative supplies, chiefly from GSA. Special mechanical aids, such as office devices, call systems, conveyor systems, new applications of automatic data processing equipment, and communications systems, are purchased after development in VA headquarters. The major categories of products VA purchases are medical, dental and hospital equipment and supplies; nuclear medical and X-ray equipment and supplies; physiological monitoring and diagnostic measuring equipment and supplies; subsistence items, including special dietary foods; electronic

93

equipment and devices; hospital furnishings; drugs and chemicals; recreational items; clothing; medical textiles; tools and equipment for use in occupational therapy programs; and equipment and components for plant maintenance.

Purchases are made by the VA Marketing Center, P.O. Box 76, Hines, Illinois 60141. Some items are bought by each individual VA field station.

DESIGN AND CONSTRUCTION OF VETERANS HOSPITALS

The construction of new VA hospitals and the modernization of existing hospitals is accomplished by the VA. Contracts for the production of working drawings and specifications are negotiated with private architect-engineer firms for the major portion of the VA construction program. VA usually selects firms in the general location of the proposed construction project.

Architect-engineer firms interested in being considered for design work should ask the VA for the architect-engineer questionnaire on which they can list their qualifications. The questionnaire becomes a part of the VA's architect-engineer library and is used to evaluate the capabilities of a firm for a project.

There is no competitive bidding on design contracts. The fee is negotiated, together with the time of completion, on a professional basis.

As a general rule, construction contracts for new hospitals and for major modernizations are accomplished by contract. Construction contracts are awarded to the lowest responsible bidder on the basis of competitive bids received after public advertisement.

A firm interested in bidding for a VA construction project should write to the Veterans Administration, Washington, D.C. 20420. The letter should describe the firm's qualifications, the specific kinds of jobs for which bid invitations are desired, and the locations in which the firm normally operates.

PART 5
Responsibilities of the Government supplier and contractor

COMPLIANCE WITH CONTRACTING REQUIREMENTS

Since Government procurement is based on public law, compliance with all the requirements of invitations for bids and contracts is necessary in doing business with the Government. Businessmen must recognize the seriousness of properly evaluating the conditions of invitations for bids, of submitting only bids in full accordance with their intentions, and of fulfilling all contractual obligations.

RESPONSIBLE SUPPLIERS

It is Government policy to award contracts only to responsible suppliers. Yet, the question of whether or not a prospective supplier is responsible is not always easy to answer. Many factors have to be considered. Information on some of these factors often is not available—for example, past performance in the case of newly established firms. Generally, the contracting officer should have information about the prospective supplier's plant facilities, production capabilities, testing facilities, quality control, financial status, and credit rating, in addition to information from any records of performance on previous Government contracts.

Since it is not possible to develop hard and fast rules which cover the wide variety of circumstances involved in all Government procurement, it is often necessary for the contracting officer to make his decision based on good business judgment in relation to all pertinent factors of the case. Standards to assist the contracting officer in determining whether prospective contractors are responsible are contained in Federal Procurement Regulation 1–1.310–5.

Although the contract award is normally based on a definite specification, compliance with some specifications depends upon the integrity of the supplier. Certain products embody special alloys or chemical compositions which require technical laboratory analysis to determine conformance to the specification. For products covered by performance specifications, there may be no similar product in existence with which to establish a basis for comparison. In these and other instances, the reputation of the bidder for honesty and dependability is an essential consideration in the determination of whether he is responsible.

Bidders should be aware of the importance of having the necessary past experience in producing the article required. Lack of experience may, at times, be given as the sole reason for rejecting a bidder as other than responsible.

Bidders should understand also that promptness of delivery is a qualifying factor, as previous failures in meeting delivery requirements is often a major factor in determining whether the supplier is responsible.

It is the responsibility of Government contractors and suppliers to determine that their products meet each technical requirement of the contract and specification before offering products for acceptance. This is the reason for requirement 5(e) in Standard

Form 32, General Provisions—Supply Contract, which specifies that the supplier shall provide and maintain an inspection system acceptable to the Government and shall keep records of all inspection work. The supplier is required to make all inspections and tests required by Federal or military specifications if provided in the contract.

If a small business concern, or small business production pool, meets all requirements for a specific contract award except those relating to capacity and credit, its bid would ordinarily be rejected. In those instances, the contracting officer will refer the matter to the Small Business Administration. The Small Business Administration has the authority to issue Certificates of Competency when its investigation reveals that the firm in question is competent to perform the contract. Small Business Administration certification is sent to the Government purchasing officer for award of the contract, and by law, its findings must be accepted as conclusive insofar as capacity and credit requirements of the particular contract are concerned.

For further information on Certificates of Competency, including the conditions under which they are issued, consult the Small Business Administration publication, "Purchasing and Sales Directory." This booklet is available for reference at any Small Business Administration field office. It is for sale at field offices of the Department of Commerce and by the Superintendent of Documents, U.S. Government Printing Office, Washington, D.C. 20402.

GENERAL CONTRACT PROVISIONS

All Government contracts contain specific provisions governing performance under the contract. In addition, most Government contracts contain or reference general provisions.

Standard Forms 19 and 23A contain the general provisions covering construction contracts. Standard Form 32 contains the general provisions covering conracts for supplies and services.

General provisions are often incorporated *by reference* in invitations for bids for both construction and supply contracts. Companies doing business with the Federal Government should be familiar with the general provisions applicable to the particular type of contract in which they are interested.

Federal agencies may supplement the general provisions to cover situations peculiar to the agency. These supplementary provisions may be attached to the invitation for bids or contract form, or incorporated only by reference.

Subjects covered in the general provisions of supply contracts include variations in quantity, inspection requirements, payments, assignment of claims, default, disputes, patents, Buy American Act, Walsh-Healey Public Contracts Act, contingent fees, and other subjects having a significant bearing on supplier performance.

Similar general provisions applicable to construction contracts include specifications and drawings, changes, changed conditions, termination for default, damages for delay, time extensions, materials and workmanship, inspection and acceptance, superintendence by the contractor, permits and responsibilities, and other pertinent conditions. In addition, construction contracts that exceed $2,000 contain Labor Standards Provisions (Standard Form 19A), which cover employment, wages, and hours of labor to be used in performance of the contract.

Provisions of general importance regarding bidding rules are included in Standard Form 22 for construction contracts and on Standard Form 33A for supply contracts.

Copies of standard forms containing general provisions are not regularly included with invitations for bids distributed to firms doing repetitive business with the Government. However, copies of these forms may be obtained from the nearest GSA Business Service Center or Government procurement office. The Appendix illustrates standard forms commonly used in Government procurement.

RESPONSIVE BIDS

It is the Government's obligation to present its requirements in exact and precise language so that prospective suppliers will be able to bid on an equal basis. The Government is also obligated to obtain its requirements only from reliable sources in order to assure satisfactory contract performance. The Government contracting officer, therefore, is required to make awards on the basis of the lowest *responsive* bid by a responsible bidder, rather than merely on the basis of the lowest bid.

Federal Procurement Regulations state that a bid shall be rejected as nonresponsive when the bid "fails to conform to the essential requirements of the invitation for bids, such as specifiations, delivery schedule, or permissible alternates thereto," or when the bidder "imposes conditions which would modify requirements of the invitation for bids or limit his liability to the Government so as to give him an advantage over other bidders." For example, under normal circumstances bids will be rejected if a bidder responds to an invitation for bids with a notice that his product is subject to prior sale, or that prices are subject to change without notice. Bids will also be rejected as nonresponsive if a bidder fails to give a definite price and instead states, "Prices in effect at time of delivery."

PREPARING THE BID

After the supplier has considered his ability to meet the requirements and conditions of the invitation for bids and all other factors which would qualify him as a responsible bidder, he should prepare his bid with the following checklist of questions in mind:

1. Has every question been fully and accurately answered and all requested information been furnished?
2. Are all the requirements of the basic specification understood?

Have requirements contained in other specifications referenced in the invitation to bid been checked, including requirements for packaging and marking?

3. Have computations of the bid price been checked and rechecked and has the price quoted been verified as accurate and complete?

4. Has due consideration been given to likely market conditions in the period in which performance will occur under the contract terms? Is the cost of raw materials rising? Are labor costs increasing? Are transportation costs a factor?

5. Can delivery requirements of the invitation be met?

6. Has the bid form been proofread after typing to be certain that no figures have been transposed or other typographical errors made?

7. Has the bid been signed?

8. Will the bid be mailed in time for receipt prior to the established deadline for opening of bids?

MISTAKES IN BIDS

Numerous examples could be cited to emphasize the importance of the various precautions listed above. Errors occur quite often in the computation or recording of bid prices. If the error causes the bid to be too low, it may result in a substantial loss by the supplier; if too high, the bidder will probably fail to obtain the contract award. In many instances, suppliers fail to allow for increased costs of raw materials, labor, or transportation, with serious losses resulting when they are required to abide by the terms of the contract.

Government regulations specify that a reasonable period of time must be allowed for the preparation and submission of bids. Because of urgent needs, this period may require immediate action by the bidder, even though it seems inadequate. These situations are no more unusual than comparable situations that occur in commercial purchasing. Close attention must be given to the deadline for submitting bids since late bids ordinarily cannot be considered.

It may seem to some bidders that policies and regulations which control Government awards and contract administration are too strict, and do not permit sufficient latitude for a contracting officer to overlook certain errors and oversights. The Government contracting officer cannot disregard the laws and regulations which control his purchasing activities. Since the contracting officer is responsible for protecting the expenditure of public funds, his actions are subject to review by the Comptroller General of the United States. Government regulations in confformity with Comptroller General decisions prescribe the criteria used by contracting officers in considering mistake cases.

Although errors in bids often result in eliminating the bid from consideration, the Comptroller General has held that in instances such as obvious errors the bid should be corrected and considered along with other bids. Instances of obvious error have included misplaced decimal points, transposed figures, and price quotation when the delivered price at destination was less than the price at the factory.

When errors are found which have a bearing on the award of the contract, it is the usual policy for the contracting officer to request verification of the bid before making the award. A recent Comptroller General decision held that the bidder should be given some indication of the general area of the bid which requires verification, such as price or delivery.

The fact that errors usually result in rejection of the bid, or in lengthy delays and increased administrative costs, it is much better to verify the complete accuracy of the bid before mailing. From the bidder's standpoint, errors may result in his having to perform in accordance with the offer, which may often entail a substantial loss.

Bidders should realize that while Government regulations are designed to permit equitable treatment for all prospective suppliers, their primary purpose is to protect the Government's interest.

NOTIFICATION OF CONTRACT AWARDS

Some agencies, including GSA, make personal delivery of the notice of contract award to suppliers at their plants. The purpose of this type of visit is to explain the supplier's responsibilities under the contract, discuss his ability to meet the contract requirements, develop questions and problem areas in connection with administration of the contract and explain the type of assistance which the agency can offer. GSA regulations specify that these visits shall normally be limited to contracts in excess of $50,000 which involve new suppliers, new types of contracts, important changes in specifications or test methods, or suppliers who have rendered substandard performances under previous contracts.

Normally, however, notice of award is mailed to the supplier, and it is his responsibility to proceed according to instructions and contract requirements. The supplier may, of course, discuss any questions and problems regarding the contract with the contracting officer, and it is strongly recommended that he do so before beginning production, for the mutual benefit of all parties concerned. If his company employs legal counsel, the supplier should verify that his lawyers are familiar with the pitfalls and peculiarities of Government contracts. In most instances the Government contracting officer will go out of his way to explain contract provisions and advise the supplier or his lawyer. It should be understood, however, that Government employees are prohibited by law from assisting a supplier in the prosecution of claims against the Government.

TERMINATION OF CONTRACTS

It is part of the Government contracting officer's normal duties to maintain a constant review of the performance of suppliers with whom contracts are placed. When nonconformance with specifications or contract requirements is discovered, the contracting officer will attempt to work out an acceptable solution

·with the supplier. When this cannot be done, it is often necessary to terminate the supplier's right to deliver under the contract and obtain a different supplier. If the contract with the new supplier involves a higher cost, the original supplier can be held liable for the difference.

The possibility of termination is one of the major reasons why the supplier, in submitting his bid, should be certain of his ability to perform in accordance with the requirements of the basic specification, referenced specifications, and the conditions and requirements of the invitation for bids and the contract. If his bid is too low, he not only may lose any profit but he may incur a substantial loss. If his contract is terminated and another supplier is obtained, he is liable for the difference in costs.

SUPPLYING NEW ITEMS

When a supplier contracts to supply a product which is related to articles he is currently producing, but which involves different parts, construction, and production techniques, he should be very thorough in verifying his costs and ability to satisfy specification requirements. The same statement is true for production of an entirely new product. When a manufacturer is bidding on a product which requires better quality materials and workmanship than has been his custom to produce, he should be certain of the total costs involved.

Many examples in Government files indicate the danger of reliance upon suppliers who have not had previous experience in producing the exact product required. Some suppliers are prone to overestimate the capabilities of their facilities to produce "different" products at the agreed-upon price, or within the required time limitations. One supplier, for instance, found that his actual costs for producing an item in conformance with the specification were $14, when he had contracted to supply the item for $9. These cases illustrate the need for caution on the part of the supplier.

INSPECTION

Suppliers doing business with the Government should realize that the supplies, equipment, and commodities they offer will be inspected before acceptance. This action is legally required because the Government must be assured that the items offered meet each technical requirement of the specifications and other terms of the contract. If the items are rejected, the supplier's invoice will not be paid. Inspection includes required chemical, operational, and functional tests.

The place of inspection, either at origin or destination, is usually specified in the contract or purchase order. Statistical sampling procedures such as those in Military Standard 105 are generally used. The lot is accepted or rejected based on the findings in the sample.

PERFORMANCE

Suppliers should also remember that a record of their performance is a part of the contract file. Rejections, late deliveries, and other failures of performance under a contract are noted in the record. This record is reviewed by contracting officers before new awards are made and has a direct bearing on whether the supplier will be considered for any future awards.

SPECIAL TYPE CONTRACTS

The preceding paragraphs have been directed to bids and contracts in general. It is important, however, to add a few additional precautions regarding other aspects of contract administration which apply to construction or other special type contracts.

Government suppliers and contractors should:

1. Look into the possibility of changes being ordered in the specifications by the contracting officer and determine if these changes can be met by their production facilities and will not exceed the limits of their working capital; make sure that changes are ordered in writing and, if possible, cover any additional costs through a written agreement.
2. Be alert for possible patent and copyright infringement. Under many contracts the contractor must indemnify the Government against patent infringement liability arising out of the Government order, especially for commercial-type supplies.
3. Check to see that their accounting system is adequate to meet Government requirements, especially on contracts providing for price redetermination or revision based on costs.
4. Know the "disputes" procedure, and know and take advantage of the different types of administrative or judicial remedies; above all, know that they must file appeals under the "disputes" clauses within 30 days.
5. Keep records of all pertinent documents and case histories on Government contracts and comply with any contract provisions which require retention of records.
6. Become familiar with the covenant against contingent fees in connection with efforts to obtain a Government contract.
7. Notify the contracting officer immediately if Government-furnished property is unsuitable or received late.
8. Observe all time limitations. This includes a wide variety of requirements, from the submission of the bid to delivery of the product and even thereafter. Contractors and suppliers should be aware of time requirements by reading and understanding the contract, including the fine print. Every sentence is significant and is included because it covers a specific requirement.

REVISED GOVERNMENT REGULATIONS AND PUBLICATIONS

The fact that Government regulations, standards, specifications, purchasing documents, and forms are frequently revised or amended is another reason for due caution on the part of the supplier. These changes are made either to make the procurement system more efficient or to conform to changed product requirements. Federal Supply Schedule contracts and other recurring contracts that are readvertised at the close of the contract period are especially susceptible to change. The forms illustrated in the Appendix are under continuing review and subject to frequent changes. Firms interested in their use should make certain that they conform to those forms actually contained or referenced in bidding documents.

It is the responsibility of the Government supplier and contractor to be aware of these changes. Government contracting officers are always glad to explain changes in regulations and other procurement documents.

A FINAL WORD OF ADVICE

The Government offers fair and impartial treatment to all suppliers who are honest in their efforts to furnish the required quality and quantity of goods in accordance with the terms and conditions of the contract. It is important to the Government that its supply personnel give their full support and cooperation to achieving a better understanding of contractual responsibilities. It is equally important that both buyer and seller have appreciation and respect for each other's rights and privileges in order to carry on a satisfactory working relationship.

Some businessmen believe that Government contracts are a paternalistic refuge from the ills of normal commercial dealings. The Government can be, and usually is, strict in its enforcement of contract terms. On the other hand, businessmen should not feel that the Government's requirement for conformance to contract and specification provisions is unfair, and, therefore, Government contracts should be avoided. Thousands of small business firms obtain Government contracts and continue to seek

Government contracts because profits and contract relationships are satisfactory. "Set-asides" and other special privileges are available for small businesses to assure them a fair share of Government procurement.

PART **6**
   How to buy
   Government-
   owned real and
   personal property

SALES OF PERSONAL PROPERTY

A wide variety of personal property no longer needed by agencies of the Federal Government is periodically placed on public sale.

The Department of Defense and GSA are the principal Government sales outlets for surplus property. As items become available for public sale, catalogs and other types of announcements are distributed to persons who have expressed an interest in bidding on the types of property being offered. In addition, public notice of the sale is provided in several ways. Sales generally are on a competitive bid basis, with the property being sold to the highest bidders whose bids are responsive to the invitation and are acceptable to the Government, prices and other factors considered.

Among the many thousands of items sold are automotive and other vehicles, aircraft, hardware, plumbing and heating equipment, paper products, office supplies and equipment, drugs and medical items, wearing apparel, textiles, and industrial equipment.

Property offered for sale may be used or unused. It may be in excellent condition, it may require minor or extensive repair, or it may have value only for its material content and be offered for sale as scrap.

Sales of surplus property of the Department of Defense are under the jurisdiction of the Defense Logistics Services Center, which maintains 10 Defense Surplus Sales Offices throughout the United States. Department of Defense surplus property is generally located at military installations.

With the exception of Atomic Energy Commission contractors, Tennessee Valley Authority, and Maritime Administration, which normally sell their own property, sales of surplus personal property of civil agencies are under the control of GSA. These sales may be conducted by the GSA Regional Offices (see Part III) serving the areas where the property may be located.

MAILING LISTS AND CATALOGS

Both GSA and the Department of Defense maintain mailing lists of persons interested in surplus property sales. Persons or companies on these lists are sent catalogs and other sales announcements in advance of sales and are given the opportunity to inspect the property and submit bids.

Each GSA regional office maintains a mailing list for sales of property located in the geographical area it serves. For general information about sales conducted by GSA, or to be placed on the mailing list, businessmen should write or call the Business Service Center in the area in which they are interested in bidding on personal property. Addresses of these offices are shown in Part III.

The Department of Defense maintains a centralized mailing list for the sales of its property located in the United States. The Defense Surplus Bidders Control Office, Defense Logistics

Services Center, Federal Center, Battle Creek, Michigan 49016, maintains this list.

Mailing lists are broken down by types of commodities and also by geographical areas of buyer interest. Therefore, requests for inclusion on mailing lists should include:

1. Full name of the individual or business firm;
2. Complete address;
3. Commodities or types of property desired (such as, passenger cars, construction equipment, machine tools); and
4. Geographical area in which the buyer wants to inspect and bid on property. (Because physical inspection before bidding is suggested, and transportation costs are borne by the purchaser, care should be taken to restrict the geographical area accordingly.)

Surplus property sales catalogs describe the property, indicate dates and times for inspection, and give other detailed information regarding the sale.

PUBLIC NOTICE OF SALES

In addition to sales cataglogs mailed to potential buyers appearing on mailing lists, public notice of sales may also be provided in one or more of the following ways:

(1) Through newspaper, radio or television announcements: (2) in trade journals and periodicals; (3) through notices placed in public buildings, such as post offices, town halls, administrative offices at county seats, and others; and (4) through announcement in the "Commerce Business Daily," which contains a listing of the larger current sales of personal property. (See Part I for information about subscriptions to this publication.)

GSA has published a pamphlet which describes personal property sales procedures and lists the names and locations of the principal Government organizations concerned. The pamphlet is entitled "Sale of Government Personal Property," and is available without charge from any GSA Business Service Center.

HOW PROPERTY IS SOLD

Property is generally sold on a competitive basis to the highest responsible bidders. Sales are open to the general public and property is offered in quantities calculated to encourage participation by business firms of all sizes as well as individuals.

No priorities or preferences are accorded to any group or individual in the public sale of Government personal property.

Sales Methods

The principal competitive sales methods used in Government selling are:

SEALED BID. Invitations for bids containing all sales terms and conditions, descriptions of the property, and instructions are mailed to potential buyers. Notice to the public is given through one or more of the several ways previously mentioned.

Bidders enter on the invitation for bids the prices they are willing to offer, sign, and return the form to the Government office specified, along with any deposit in acceptable form as may be required by the invitation. These bids are opened publicly on the announced date, awards are made, and successful bidders are notified.

PUBLIC AUCTION. Traditional commercial auctioning methods are followed. Catalogs which include instructions are provided potential buyers, and public notice is given in the usual manner. Services of professionally qualified auctioneers are generally used. Removal of the property is the responsibility of the buyer .

SPOT BID. Generally, the buyer writes his bid and places it in a bid box at the sale site. Successful bidders are then

116

determined and awards made for each item or lot. The buyer is responsible for removing the property he has purchased. Information regarding property for sale and instructions for placing bids are supplied to persons on mailing lists. The usual public notice is also provided. In some instances, provisions are made for prospective purchasers who cannot attend the sale in person to bid by other means.

GENERAL CONDITIONS OF SALE

Close attention should be given to the instructions provided in sales brochures and announcements concerning scheduled sales.

Bidders may be required to submit a deposit with their sealed bids, usually amounting to 20% of the total bid. For successful bidders, the sale brochure describes the steps necessary to complete payment and remove the property. Deposits are refunded promptly to unsuccessful bidders.

All bidders are urged to inspect the items on which they plan to bid since the property is offered on an ''as-is, where-is'' basis.

SALES OF REAL PROPERTY

Real property no longer required by any Federal agency is designated as surplus to the needs of the Government. The property is then available to eligible local government units and non-profit institutions. If the property cannot be utilized for non-Federal public purposes, it is generally advertised for sale on a competitive-bid basis.

GSA is the principal Government agency responsible for the sale of surplus real property to the public, although special categories of land and improvements may be offered for sale by other agencies for reasons of efficientcy, or in instances in which disposition functions are closely related to the program of the agency. For example, housing units acquired by the Government under mortgage foreclosure proceedings, in connection with GI loans, are sold by the Veterans Administration. Surplus buildings and other improvements located on land to be retained in

Government ownership are normally offered for sale by the agency having care and custody of the land.

The types of real property which GSA sells range from unimproved rural and urban land to improved commercial industrial facilities. Properties for sale include residences, office buildings, factories, and warehouses, as well as vacant land suitable for various uses, such as farming, residential development, business purposes, and manufacturing. In short, GSA sells nearly every type of real estate found on the commercial market and in many cases, buyers may utilize the properties immediately for productive purposes.

PUBLICIZING REAL PROPERTY SALES

When Government real property is to be offered for sale, the sale is publicized in a manner similar to personal property. The GSA regional office serving the area in which the property is located prepares a notice briefly describing the property and explaining how, when , and where it will be sold. The notices are mailed to prospective buyers who have previously indicated an interest in buying property similar in type, location, and value to that being offered for sale. Mailing lists for this purpose are maintained in each GSA regional office. Applications to be placed on the mailing lists may be obtained from any GSA Business Service Center.

Scheduled sales are widely publicized through advertisements and announcements in newspapers, magazines, and trade journals and through radio, television, and direct mail. Announcements of real property sales are also made in the "Commerce Business Daily." In addition, specialists are available in regional offices for consultation about properties scheduled for sale as well as properties to be offered in the future.

A booklet—"Disposal of Surplus Real Property"—is available without charge from GSA Business Service Centers. That booklet explains in detail the Government real property sales procedure as well as other phases of the real property utilization and disposal program.

SALES METHODS

GSA offers real property for sale to the general public through sealed bid invitations, public auction, and real estate brokers.

Sealed Bidding. When this method of sale is employed, the GSA regional office will mail to all prospective purchasers, upon request, an invitation for bids containing a description of the property, terms and conditions of sale, and complete instructions for bidding.

Bids are then submitted, along with the required deposit, to the regional office which issued the invitation. The bids are opened and read publicly on a specified bid-opening date at a specified time. If the highest bid is acceptable, an award is made, usually within 60 days, and the successful bidder notified. Deposits are returned promptly to all unsuccessful bidders when they are notified of the rejection of their bids.

Public Auction. Sales of surplus real property may also be conducted by qualified auctioneers. Bidders must be prepared to submit a predetermined and publicly announced earnest money deposit in a fixed amount. Award is made to the highest bidder whose offer made to the auctioneer is acceptable to the Government.

Auction sales are usually conducted on the property site; at times, they are held at a convenient location in the vicinity of the property.

Brokers. Services of realty brokers are secured by contract to supplement other GSA sales efforts. Broker services are used principally in the sale of complex industrial facilities and other special-purpose properties which require brokers' organizational capabilities, diversified clienteles, and professional affiliations, including the assistance of realtor organizations, to find prospective buyers having a need for such properties. This method of sale is used less frequently than sealed bids or auctions.

ADVICE TO PROSPECTIVE BUYERS OF REAL PROPERTY

1. Give close attention to the instructions provided in the sales brochures and announcements concerning scheduled sales.
2. Carefully inspect the property being offered for sale before bidding. It will be sold on an "as-is, where-is" basis. Lack of full information about the condition of the property will not constitute grounds for adjustment or withdrawal of bids.
3. Be prepared to submit, with bids, the earnest money deposit in the form and amount specified by the Government. Property is normally offered on a cash and/or credit basis. When credit terms are available and desired, make certain that the financial information necessary for credit approval is available. GSA generally follows commercial practices in extending credit.

DISPOSALS OF STRATEGIC AND CRITICAL MATERIALS

General policies and guidelines for the disposal of these excesses were established as a result of recommendations of the Executive Stockpile Committee report approved by the President in 1963. In accordance with recommendations in this report, an Interdepartmental Disposal Committee was established in 1963 by the Office of Emergency Planning to develop long-range programs for the disposal of excess stockpile materials by GSA.

The committee, chaired by OEP, consisted of representatives from various affected Government agencies. The work of the committee was supplemented by a subcommittee, chaired by GSA, whose responsibility it was to recommend the scope of the disposal program and guidelines as to the quantity and rate of sales and to review other pertinent factors to ensure that the interests of the domestic industries and effects on foreign governments were thoroughly taken into consideration. The subcommittee was assisted by interagency working groups which developed the necessary technical, economic, and statistical data required in arriving at the long-range disposal recommendations. The Interdepartmental Disposal Committee was disestablished in July 1967. Since that time, GSA has been responsible for continued consultations with the affected agencies and related industries on the development of disposal programs for those commodities declared excess to stockpile requirements by OEP.

As of the end of Fiscal Year 1968, a total of approximately 47 million short tons of materials was in inventories in GSA custody. These materials are stored at 143 locations in 45 States. The acquisition cost of the inventories approximates $6.962 billion. The estimated current market value is approximately $6.836 billion. Of the total inventory approximately $3.2 billion, at current market value, is excess to the current requirements of the Government.

These huge quantities of Government-owned strategic and critical materials excess to Government needs not only represent a substantial economic burden to the taxpayer, but they also constitute an everpresent uncertainty to producers and consumers who otherwise would be concerned only with the usual competitive forces of supply and demand. Emphasis is, therefore, on disposal of these excess materials by GSA. Since 1959, cumulative stockpile sales have exceeded $2.9 billion, and the contract value of disposals during Fiscal Year 1968 was $207.4 million.

In addition to potential excesses in the commodities listed on the following page, Property Management and Disposal Service also offers for sale each week two million troy ounces of silver bullion from United States Treasury stocks.

These excess materials, when authorized for disposal, are sold either by sealed bid, negotiation, or on a fixed-price basis. GSA issues periodic news releases announcing its sales programs for the various commodities that are available for sale.

Additional information concerning the availability of excess materials and methods of disposal may be obtained from the

Property Management and Disposal Service, General Services Administration, Washington, D.C. 20405.

PARTIAL LIST OF STOCKPILE ITEMS HAVING POTENTIAL EXCESS AVAILABLE FOR SALE

Aluminum
Aluminum Oxide
Antimony
Asbestos, Amosite
Asbestos, Chrysotile
Asbestos, Crocidolite
Beryl
Bismuth
Cadmium
Castor Oil
Celestite
Chromite, Chemical Grade
Chromite, Metallurgical Grade
Cobalt
Columbium
Cordage Fiber, Abaca
Cordage Fiber, Sisal
Diamonds, Industrial Stones
Fluorspar, Acid Grade
Graphite, Natural Malagasy, Crystalline
Graphite, Natural, Other Than C & M Crystalline
Magnesium
Manganese, Metallurgical Grade
Mercury
Mica, Muscovite Stained and Better
Mica, Muscovite Stained B and Lower

Mica, Muscovite Film 1st and 2nd Qualities
Mica, Muscovite Film Third Quality
Mica, Muscovite Splittings
Mica, Phlogopite Block
Mica, Phlogopite Splittings
Molybdenum
Platinum Group Metals—Ruthenium
Quartz Crystals.
Rare Earths
Rubber
Shellac
Talc, Steatite Block & Lump
Talc, Steatite Ground
Tin
Titanium Sponge
Tungsten
Vanadium
Vegetable Tannin Entract —Chestnut
Vegetable Tannin Extract —Quebracho
Vegetable Tannin Extract —Wattle
Zinc
Zirconium Ore, Baddeleyite
Zirconium Ore, Zircon

APPENDIX
Standard forms commonly used in Government procurement

STANDARD FORM 19 DECEMBER 1965 EDITION GENERAL SERVICES ADMINISTRATION FED. PROC. REG. (41 CFR) 1—16.401	**INVITATION, BID, AND AWARD** (Construction, Alteration or Repair) ☐ CHECK IF SMALL BUSINESS SET-ASIDE OR OTHER NEGOTIATED PROCUREMENT *(If checked, "Bid" includes "Proposal")*	REFERENCE *(Include in correspondence)*

INVITATION FOR BIDS	DATE ISSUED:

ISSUING OFFICE *	BID RECEIVING OFFICE *

Information regarding bidding material may be obtained from the issuing office.

SEALED BIDS in   covering work described in specifications, schedules, drawings and conditions
entitled and dated as follows:

will be received at the Bid Receiving Office until _____   _____
and at that time publicly opened.   *(Hour and Time Zone)*   *(Date)*

Sealed envelopes containing bids shall be addressed to the Bid Receiving Office and shall be marked to show: Bidder's Name and
Address; * Reference   ; Time and Date of Opening;

BID *(This Section to be completed by Bidder)*	➤ DATE BID SUBMITTED:

The undersigned agrees, if this bid is accepted within   calendar days *(30 days unless a different period is inserted)* after date
of opening, to complete all work specified in strict accordance with the above-identified documents and the General Provisions on the
reverse hereof, within   calendar days after receipt of notice to proceed, for the following amount_____

including all applicable Federal, State, and local taxes. The undersigned further agrees, if any contract award resulting from this bid
exceeds $2,000, TO COMPLY with the provisions of Standard Form 19-A, Labor Standards Provisions Applicable to Contracts in
Excess of $2,000 and TO FURNISH a performance bond in an amount equal to 100 percent and a payment bond in an amount equal
to 50 percent of the contract price with surety or sureties acceptable to the Government, on Government forms within   days
after forms are furnished.

The representations and certifications on the accompanying STANDARD FORM 19-B are made a
part of this bid.

NAME AND ADDRESS OF BIDDER *(Street, city, State)* * *(Type or print.)*	SIGNATURE OF PERSON AUTHORIZED TO SIGN THIS BID ➤ SIGNER'S NAME AND TITLE *(Type or print.)*

AWARD *(This Section for Government only)*	DATE OF AWARD:

THE ABOVE BID IS ACCEPTED IN THE AMOUNT OF $
☐ YOU ARE DIRECTED TO PROCEED WITH THE WORK UPON RECEIPT OF THIS AWARD.
☐ NOTICE TO PROCEED WILL BE ISSUED UPON RECEIPT OF ACCEPTABLE PAYMENT AND PERFORMANCE BONDS.

	THE UNITED STATES OF AMERICA
	
	BY _____
	           (Contracting Officer)
	
	_____
	           (Title)

*Include "ZIP CODE" in all mailing addresses.   19–110

1. **CHANGES AND CHANGED CONDITIONS**

   (a) The Contracting Officer may, in writing, order changes in the drawings and specifications within the general scope of the contract.

   (b) The Contractor shall promptly notify the Contracting Officer in writing of subsurface or latent physical conditions differing materially from those indicated in this contract or unknown unusual physical conditions at the site, before proceeding further with the work.

   (c) If changes under (a) or conditions under (b) increase or decrease the cost of, or time required for, performing the work, upon assertion of a claim by the Contractor before final payment under the contract, a written equitable adjustment shall be made; except that no adjustment under (b) shall be made unless the notice required therein was given or unless the Contracting Officer waives the requirement therefor. If the adjustment cannot be agreed upon, the dispute shall be decided pursuant to Clause 3.

2. **TERMINATION FOR DEFAULT—DAMAGES FOR DELAY— TIME EXTENSIONS**

   (a) If the Contractor does not prosecute the work so as to insure completion, or fails to complete it, within the time specified, the Government may, by written notice to the Contractor, terminate his right to proceed. Thereafter, the Government may have the work completed and the Contractor shall be liable for any resulting excess cost to the Government. If the Government does not terminate the Contractor's right to proceed, he shall continue the work and shall be liable to the Government for any actual damages occasioned by such delay unless liquidated damages are stipulated.

   (b) The Contractor's right to proceed shall not be terminated nor the Contractor charged with actual or liquidated damages under (a) above because of any delays in completion of the work due to causes other than normal weather, beyond his control and without his fault or negligence, including but not restricted to, acts of God, acts of the public enemy, acts of the Government (in either its sovereign or contractual capacity), acts of another contractor in the performance of a contract with the Government, fires, floods, epidemics, quarantine restrictions, strikes, freight embargoes, and unusually severe weather, or delays of subcontractors or suppliers due to causes beyond their control and without their fault or negligence: Provided, That the Contractor shall within 10 days from the beginning of any such delay, unless the Contracting Officer shall grant a further period of time prior to the date of final payment under the contract, notify the Contracting Officer in writing of the causes of delay and the facts relating thereto. The Contracting Officer shall consider the facts and ascertain the extent of the delay, and extend the time for completing the work when in his judgment the facts justify such an extension, and his decision shall be final and conclusive on the parties, subject only to appeal as provided in Clause 3.

3. **DISPUTES**

   Any dispute concerning a question of fact arising under this contract, not disposed of by agreement, shall be decided by the Contracting Officer, who shall reduce his decision to writing and furnish a signed copy to the Contractor. Such decision shall be final and conclusive unless, within 30 days from the date of receipt thereof, the Contractor mails or otherwise furnishes to the Contracting Officer a written appeal, addressed to the head of the Federal agency. The Contractor shall be afforded an opportunity to be heard and to offer evidence. The decision of the head of the Federal agency or his authorized representative, shall be final and conclusive unless fraudulent, or capricious, or arbitrary, or so grossly erroneous as necessarily to imply bad faith, or not supported by substantial evidence. Pending final decision of a dispute hereunder, the Contractor shall proceed diligently with the performance of the contract and in accordance with the Contracting Officer's decision.

4. **RESPONSIBILITY OF CONTRACTOR**

   At his own expense the Contractor shall: (a) obtain any necessary licenses and permits; (b) provide competent superintendence; (c) take precautions necessary to protect persons or property against injury or damage and be responsible for any such injury or damage that occurs as a result of his fault or negligence; (d) perform the work without unnecessarily interfering with other contractors' work or Government activities; (e) be responsible for all damage to work performed and materials delivered (including Government-furnished items), until completion and final acceptance.

5. **MATERIAL AND WORKMANSHIP**

   All material incorporated in the work shall be new and the work shall be performed in a skillful and workmanlike manner. Both materials and workmanship shall be subject to the inspection of the Contracting Officer or his duly authorized representative who may require the Contractor to correct defective workmanship or materials without cost to the Government.

6. **PAYMENTS TO CONTRACTOR**

   Progress payments equal to 90 percent of the value of work performed may be made monthly on estimates approved by the Contracting Officer. Upon payment therefor, title to the property shall vest in the Government. The Contractor will notify the Government when all work is complete. Final payment will be made after final acceptance.

7. **OFFICIALS NOT TO BENEFIT**

   No Member of or Delegate to Congress, or Resident Commissioner, shall be admitted to any share or part of this contract, or to any benefit that may arise therefrom; but this provision shall not be construed to extend to this contract if made with a corporation for its general benefit.

8. **BUY AMERICAN**

   The Contractor, subcontractors, material men, and suppliers must comply with the Buy American Act of March 3, 1933 (41 U.S.C. 10a–10d) and Executive Order 10582 of December 17, 1954 (19 Fed. Reg. 8723). (In substance the above require use generally of domestic materials except as otherwise authorized by the Contracting Officer pursuant to the Act and Executive Order.)

9. **ASSIGNMENT OF CLAIMS**

   If this contract provides for payments aggregating $1,000 or more, claims for moneys due or to become due hereunder may be assigned as provided in 31 U.S.C. 203 and 41 U.S.C. 15.

10. **CONVICT LABOR**

    In connection with the performance of work under this contract, the Contractor agrees not to employ any person undergoing sentence of imprisonment at hard labor.

11. **COVENANT AGAINST CONTINGENT FEES**

    The Contractor warrants that no person or selling agency has been employed or retained to solicit or secure this contract upon an agreement or understanding for a commission, percentage, brokerage, or contingent fee, excepting bona fide employees or bona fide established commercial or selling agencies maintained by the Contractor for the purpose of securing business. For breach or violation of this warranty the Government shall have the right to annul this contract without liability or in its discretion to deduct from the contract price or consideration, or otherwise recover, the full amount of such commission, percentage, brokerage, or contingent fee.

12. **EXAMINATION OF RECORDS**

    (*The following clause is applicable if this contract exceeds $2,500 and was entered into by means of negotiation, but is not applicable if entered into by means of formal advertising.*)

    (a) The Contractor agrees that the Comptroller General of the United States or any of his duly authorized representatives shall, until the expiration of three years after final payment under this contract, have access to and the right to examine any directly pertinent books, documents, papers, and records of the Contractor involving transactions related to this contract.

    (b) The Contractor further agrees to include in all his subcontracts hereunder a provision to the effect that the subcontractor agrees that the Comptroller General of the United States or any of his duly authorized representatives shall, until the expiration of three years after final payment under the subcontract, have access to and the right to examine any directly pertinent books, documents, papers, and records of such subcontractor, involving transactions related to the subcontract. The term "subcontract" as used in this clause excludes (i) purchase orders not exceeding $2,500 and (ii) subcontracts or purchase orders for public utility services at rates established for uniform applicability to the general public.

13. **UTILIZATION OF SMALL BUSINESS CONCERNS**

    (*The following clause is applicable if this contract exceeds $5,000.*)

    (a) It is the policy of the Government as declared by the Congress that a fair proportion of the purchases and contracts for supplies and services for the Government be placed with small business concerns.

    (b) The Contractor agrees to accomplish the maximum amount of subcontracting to small business concerns that the Contractor finds to be consistent with the efficient performance of this contract.

STANDARD FORM 21
DECEMBER 1965 EDITION
GENERAL SERVICES ADMINISTRATION
FED. PROC. REG. (41 CFR) 1-16.401

BID FORM
(CONSTRUCTION CONTRACT)

REFERENCE

Read the Instructions to Bidders (Standard Form 22)
This form to be submitted in

DATE OF INVITATION

NAME AND LOCATION OF PROJECT

NAME OF BIDDER *(Type or print)*

(Date)

TO:

In compliance with the above-dated invitation for bids, the undersigned hereby proposes to perform all work for

in strict accordance with the General Provisions (Standard Form 23-A), Labor Standards Provisions Applicable to Contracts in Excess of $2,000 (Standard Form 19-A), specifications, schedules, drawings, and conditions, for the following amount(s)

21-108

(Continue on other side)

The undersigned agrees that, upon written acceptance of this bid, mailed or otherwise furnished within   calendar days (calendar days unless a different period be inserted by the bidder) after the date of opening of bids, he will within   calendar days (unless a longer period is allowed) after receipt of the prescribed forms, execute Standard Form 23, Construction Contract, and give performance and payment bonds on Government standard forms with good and sufficient surety.

The undersigned agrees, if awarded the contract, to commence the work within   calendar days after the date of receipt of notice to proceed, and to complete the work within   calendar days after the date of receipt of notice to proceed.

RECEIPT OF AMENDMENTS: *The undersigned acknowledges receipt of the following amendments of the invitation for bids, drawings, and/or specifications, etc. (Give number and date of each):*

The representations and certifications on the accompanying STANDARD FORM 19-B are made a part of this bid.

ENCLOSED IS BID GUARANTEE, CONSISTING OF	IN THE AMOUNT OF

NAME OF BIDDER (*Type or print*)	FULL NAME OF ALL PARTNERS (*Type or print*)
BUSINESS ADDRESS (*Type or print*) (*Include "ZIP Code"*)	
BY (*Signature in ink. Type or print name under signature*)	
TITLE (*Type or print*)	

DIRECTIONS FOR SUBMITTING BIDS: *Envelopes containing bids, guarantee, etc., must be sealed, marked, and addressed as follows:*

CAUTION—Bids should not be qualified by exceptions to the bidding conditions.

Taken From
STANDARD FORM 22
JUNE 1964 EDITION
GENERAL SERVICES ADMINISTRATION
FED. PROC. REG. (41 CFR) 1–16.401

INSTRUCTIONS TO BIDDERS
(CONSTRUCTION CONTRACT)

1. **Explanations to Bidders.** Any explanation desired by a bidder regarding the meaning or interpretation of the invitation for bids, drawings, specifications, etc., must be requested in writing and with sufficient time allowed for a reply to reach bidders before the submission of their bids. Any interpretation made will be in the form of an amendment of the invitation for bids, drawings, specifications, etc., and will be furnished to all prospective bidders. Its receipt by the bidder must be acknowledged in the space provided on the Bid Form (Standard Form 21) or by letter or telegram received before the time set for opening of bids. Oral explanations or instructions given before the award of the contract will not be binding.

2. **Conditions Affecting the Work.** Bidders should visit the site and take such other steps as may be reasonably necessary to ascertain the nature and location of the work, and the general and local conditions which can affect the work or the cost thereof. Failure to do so will not relieve bidders from responsibility for estimating properly the difficulty or cost of successfully performing the work. The Government will assume no responsibility for any understanding or representations concerning conditions made by any of its officers or agents prior to the execution of the contract, unless included in the invitation for bids, the specifications, or related documents.

3. **Bidder's Qualifications.** Before a bid is considered proper award, the bidder may be requested by the Government to submit a statement regarding his previous experience in performing comparable work, his business and technical organization, financial resources, and plant available to be used in performing the work.

4. Bid Guarantee. Where a bid guarantee is required by the invitation for bids, failure to furnish a bid guarantee in the proper form and amount, by the time set for opening of bids, may be cause for rejection of the bid.

A bid guarantee shall be in the form of a firm commitment, such as a bid bond, postal money order, certified check, cashier's check, irrevocable letter of credit or, in accordance with Treasury Department regulations, certain bonds or notes of the United States. Bid guarantees, other than bid bonds, will be returned (a) to unsuccessful bidders as soon as practicable after the opening of bids, and (b) to the successful bidder upon execution of such further contractual documents and bonds as may be required by the bid as accepted.

If the successful bidder, upon acceptance of his bid by the Government within the period specified therein for acceptance (sixty days if no period is specified) fails to execute such further contractual documents, if any, and give such bond(s) as may be required by the terms of the bid as accepted within the time specified (ten days if no period is specified) after receipt of the forms by him, his contract may be terminated for default. In such event he shall be liable for any cost of procuring the work which exceeds the amount of his bid, and the bid guarantee shall be available toward offsetting such difference.

5. Preparation of Bids. (a) Bids shall be submitted on the forms furnished, or copies thereof, and must be manually signed. If erasures or other changes appear on the forms, each erasure or change must be initialed by the person signing the bid. Unless specifically authorized in the invitation for bids, telegraphic bids will not be considered.

(b) The bid form may provide for submission of a price or prices for one or more items, which may be lump sum bids, alternate prices, scheduled items resulting in a bid on a unit of construction or a combination thereof, etc. Where the bid form explicitly requires that the bidder bid on all items, failure to do so will disqualify the bid. When submission of a pirce on all items is not required, bidders should insert the words "no bid" in the space provided for any item on which no price is submitted.

(c) Unless called for, alternate bids will not be considered.

(d) Modifications of bids already submitted will be considered if received at the office designated in the invitation for bids by the time set for opening of bids. Telegraphic modifications will be considered, but should not reveal the amount of the original or revised bid.

6. Submission of Bids. Bids must be sealed, marked, and addressed as directed in the invitation for bids. Failure to do so may result in a premature opening of, or a failure to open, such bid.

7. Late Bids and Modifications or Withdrawals. (a) Bids and modifications or withdrawals thereof received at the office designated in the invitation for bids after the exact time set for opening of bids will not be considered unless : (1) They are received before award is made; and either (2) they are sent by registered mail or by certified mail for which an official dated post office stamp (postmark) on the original Receipt for Certified Mail has been obtained, or by telegraph if authorized, and it is determined by the Government that the late receipt was due solely to delay in the mails, or delay by the telegraph company, for which the bidder was not responbible; or (3) if submitted by mail (or by telegram if authorized), it is determined by the Government that the late receipt was due solely to mishandling by the Government after receipt at the Government installation : *Provided,* That timely receipt at such installation is established upon examination of an appropriate date or time stamp (if any) of such installation, or of other documentary evidence of receipt (if readily available) within the control of such installation or of the post office serving it. However, a modification which makes the terms of the otherwise successful bid more favorable to the Government will be considered at any time it is received and may thereafter be accepted.

(b) Bidders using certified mail are cautioned to obtain a Receipt for Certified Mail showing a legible, dated postmark and to retain such receipt against the chance that it will be required as evidence that a late bid was timely mailed.

(c) The time of mailing of late bids submitted by registered or certified mail shall be deemed to be the last minute of the date shown in the postmark on the registered mail receipt or registered mail wrapper or on the Receipt for Certified Mail unless the bidder furnishes evidence from the post office station of mailing which establishes an earlier time. In the case of certified mail, the only acceptable evidence is as follows: (1) where the Receipt for Certified Mail identifies the post office station of mailing, evidence furnished by the bidder which establishes that the business day of that station ended at an earlier time, in which case the time of mailing shall be deemed to be the last minute of the business day of that station; or (2) an entry in ink on the Receipt for Certified Mail showing the time of mailing and the initials of the postal employee receiving the item and making the entry, with appropriate written verification of such entry from the post office station of mailing, in which case the time of mailing shall be the time shown in the entry. If the postmark on the original Receipt for Certified Mail does not show a date, the bid shall not be considered.

8. Withdrawal of Bids. Bids may be withdrawn by written or telegraphic request received from bidders prior to the time set for opening of bids.

9. Public Opening of Bids. Bids will be publicly opened at the time set for opening in the invitation for bids. There content will be made public for the information of bidders and others interested, who may be present either in person or by representative.

10. Award of Contract. (*a*) Award of contract will be made to that responsible bidder whose bid, conforming to the invitation for bids, is most advantageous to the Government, price and other factors considered.

(*b*) The Government may, when in its interest, reject any or all bids or waive any informality in bids received.

(*c*) The Government may accept any item or combination of items of a bid, unless precluded by the invitation for bids or the bidder includes in his bid a restrictive limitation.

11. Contract and Bonds. The bidder whose bid is accepted will, within the time established in the bid, enter into a written contract with the Government and, if required, furnish performance and payment bonds on Government standard forms in the amounts indicated in the invitation for bids or the specifications.

131

STANDARD FORM 23
JANUARY 1961 EDITION
GENERAL SERVICES ADMINISTRATION
FED. PROC. REG. (41 CFR) 1-16 401

CONSTRUCTION CONTRACT
(See instructions on reverse)

CONTRACT NO

DATE OF CONTRACT

NAME AND ADDRESS OF CONTRACTOR

CHECK APPROPRIATE BOX

☐ Individual
☐ Partnership
☐ Joint Venture
☐ Corporation, incorporated in the
State of _____.

DEPARTMENT OR AGENCY

CONTRACT FOR *(Work to be performed)*

PLACE

CONTRACT PRICE *(Express in words and figures)*

ADMINISTRATIVE DATA *(Optional)*

The United States of America (hereinafter called the Government), represented by the Contracting Officer executing this contract, and the individual, partnership, joint venture, or corporation named above (hereinafter called the Contractor), mutually agree to perform this contract in strict accordance with the General Provisions (Standard Form 23-A), Labor Standards Provisions Applicable to Contracts in Excess of $2,000 (Standard Form 19-A), and the following designated specifications, schedules, drawings, and conditions:

WORK SHALL BE STARTED

WORK SHALL BE COMPLETED

Alterations.   The following alterations were made in this contract before it was signed by the parties hereto:

In witness whereof, the parties hereto have executed this contract as of the date entered on the first page hereof.

THE UNITED STATES OF AMERICA   CONTRACTOR

By _____   _____
                                                                    (Name of Contractor)

_____   By _____
            (Official title)   *(Signature)*

                                                    _____
                                                                    (Title)

INSTRUCTIONS

1. The full name and business address of the Contractor must be inserted in the space provided on the face of the form. The Contractor shall sign in the space provided above with his usual signature and typewrite or print his name under the signature.

2. An officer of a corporation, a member of a partnership, or an agent signing for the Contractor shall place his signature and title after the word "By" under the name of the Contractor. A contract executed by an attorney or agent on behalf of the Contractor shall be accompanied by two authenticated copies of his power of attorney or other evidence of his authority to act on behalf of the Contractor.

Taken From
STANDARD FORM 23-A
JUNE 1964 EDITION
GENERAL SERVICES ADMINISTRATION
FED. PROC. REG. (41 CFR) 1-16.401

GENERAL PROVISIONS
(Construction Contract)

1. DEFINITIONS

(a) The term "head of the agency" or "Secretary" as used herein means the Secretary, the Under Secretary, any Assistant Secretary, or any other head or assistant head of the executive or military department or other Federal agency; and the term "his duly authorized representative" means any person or persons or board (other than the Contracting Officer) authorized to act for the head of the agency or the Secretary.

(b) The term "Contracting Officer" as used herein means the person executing this contract on behalf of the Government and includes a duly appointed successor or authorized representative.

2. SPECIFICATIONS AND DRAWINGS

The Contractor shall keep on the work a copy of the drawings and specifications and shall at all times give the Contracting Officer access thereto. Anything mentioned in the specifications and not shown on the drawings, or shown on the drawings and not mentioned in the specifications, shall be of like effect as if shown or mentioned in both. In case of difference between drawings and specifications, the specifications shall govern. In case of discrepancy either in the figures, in the drawings, or in the specifications, the matter shall be promptly submitted to the Contracting Officer, who shall promptly make a determination in writing. Any adjustment by the Contractor without such a determination shall be at his own risk and expense. The Contracting Officer shall furnish from time to time such detail drawings and other information as he may consider necessary, unless otherwise provided.

3. CHANGES

The Contracting Officer may, at any time, by written order, and without notice to the sureties, make changes in the drawings and/or specifications of this contract if within its general scope. If such changes cause an increase or decrease in the Contractor's cost of, or. time required for, performance of the contract, an equitable adjustment shall be made and the contract modified in writing accordingly. Any claim of the Contractor for adjustment under this clause must be asserted in writing within 30 days from the date of receipt by the Contractor of the notification of change unless the Contracting Officer grants a further period of time before the date of final payment under the contract. If the parties fail to agree upon the adjustment to be made, the dispute shall be determined as provided in Clause 6 of these General Provisions; but nothing provided in this clause shall excuse the Contractor from proceeding with the prosecution of the work as changed. Except as otherwise provided in this contract, no charge for any extra work or material will be allowed.

4. CHANGED CONDITIONS

The Contractor shall promptly, and before such conditions are disturbed, notify the Contracting Officer in writing of: (a) subsurface or latent physical conditions at the site differing materially from those indicated in this contract, or (b) unknown physical conditions at the site, of an unusual nature, differing materially from those ordinarily

134

encountered and generally recognized as inhering in work of the character provided for in this contract. The Contracting Officer shall promptly investigate the conditions, and if he finds that such conditions do so materially differ and cause an increase or decrease in the Contractor's cost of, or the time required for, performance of this contract, an equitable adjustment shall be made and the contract modified in writing accordingly. Any claim of the Contractor for adjustment hereunder shall not be allowed unless he has given notice as above required; or unless the Contracting Officer grants a further period of time before the date of final payment under the contract. If the parties fail to agree upon the adjustment to be made, the dispute shall be determined as provided in Clause 6 of these General Provisions.

5. TERMINATION FOR DEFAULT—DAMAGES FOR DELAY—TIME EXTENSIONS

(a) If the Contractor refuses or fails to prosecute the work, or any separable part thereof, with such diligence as will insure its completion within the time specified in this contract, or any extension thereof, or fails to complete said work within such time, the Government may, by written notice to the Contractor, terminate his right to proceed with the work or such part of the work as to which there has been delay. In such event the Government may take over the work and prosecute the same to completion, by contract or otherwise, and may take possession of and utilize in completing the work such materials, appliances, and plant as may be on the site of the work and necessary therefor. Whether or not the Contractor's right to proceed with the work is terminated, he and his sureties shall be liable for any damage to the Government resulting from his refusal or failure to complete the work within the specified time.

(b) If fixed and agreed liquidated damages are provided in the contract and if the Government so terminates the Contractor's right to proceed, the resulting damage will consist of such liquidated damages until such reasonable time as may be required for final completion of the work together with any increased costs occasioned the Government in completing the work.

(c) If fixed and agreed liquidated damages are provided in the contract and if the Government does not so terminate the Contractor's right to proceed, the resulting damage will consist of such liquidated damages until the work is completed or accepted.

(d) The Contractor's right to proceed shall not be so terminated nor the Contractor charged with resulting damage if:

(1) The delay in the completion of the work arises from unforeseeable causes beyond the control and without the fault or negligence of the Contractor, including but not restricted to, acts of God, acts of the public enemy, acts of the Government in either its soverign or contractual capacity, acts of another contractor in the performance of a contract with the Government, fires, floods, epidemics, quarantine restrictions, strikes, freight embargoes, unusually severe weather, or delays of subcontractors or suppliers arising from unforeseeable causes beyond the control and without the fault or negligence of both the Contractor and such subcontractors or suppliers; and

(2) The Contractor, within 10 days from the beginning of any such delay (unless the Contracting Officer grants a further period of time before the date of final payment under the contract), notifies the Contracting Officer in writing of the causes of delay. The Contracting Officer shall ascertain the facts and the extent of the delay and extend the time for completing the work when, in his judgment, the findings of fact justify such an extension, and his findings of fact shall be final and conclusive on the parties, subject only to appeal as provided in Clause 6 of these General Provisions.

(e) If, after notice of termination of the Contractor's right to proceed under the provisions of this clause, it is determined for any reason that the Contractor was not in default under the provisions of this clause, or that the delay was excusable under the provisions of this clause, the rights and obligations of the parties shall, if the contract contains a clause providing for termination for convenience of the Government, be the same as if the notice of termination had been issued pursuant to such clause. If, in the foregoing circumstances, this contract does not contain a clause providing for termination for convenience of the Government, the contract shall be equitably adjusted to compensate for such termination and the contract modified accordingly; failure to agree to any such adjustment shall be a dispute concerning a question of fact within the meaining of the clause of this contract entitled "Disputes."

(f) The rights and remedies of the Government provided in this clause are in addition to any other rights and remedies provided by law or under this contract.

6. DISPUTES

(a) Except as otherwise provided in this contract, any dispute concerning a question of fact arising under this contract which is not disposed of by agreement shall be decided by the Contracting Officer, who shall reduce his decision to writing and mail or otherwise furnish a copy thereof to the Contractor. The decision of the Contracting Officer shall be final and conclusive unless, within 30 days from the date of receipt of such copy, the Contractor mails or otherwise furnishes to the Contracting Officer a wirtten appeal addressed to the head of the agency involved. The decision of the head of the agency or his duly authorized representative for the determination of such appeals shall be final and conclusive. This provision shall not be pleaded in any suit involving a question of fact arising under this contract as limiting judicial review of any such decision to cases where fraud by such official or his representative or board is alleged: *Provided, however,* that any such decision shall be final and conclusive unless the same is fraudulent or capricious or arbitrary or so grossly erroneous as necessarily to imply bad faith or is not supported by substantial evidence. In connection with any appeal proceeding under this clause, the Contractor shall be afforded an opportunity to be heard and to offer evidence in support of his appeal. Pending final decision of a dispute hereunder, the Contractor shall proceed diligently with the performance of the contract and in accordance with the Contracting Officer's decision.

(b) This Disputes clause does not preclude consideration of questions of law in connection with decisions provided for in paragraph (a) above. Nothing in this contract, however, shall be construed as making final the decision of any administrative official, representative, or board on a question of law.

7. PAYMENTS TO CONTRACTOR

(a) The Government will pay the contract price as hereinafter provided.

(b) The Government will make progress payments monthly as the work proceeds, or at more frequent intervals as determined by the Contracting Officer, on estimates approved by the Contracting Officer. If requested by the Contracting Officer, the Contractor shall furnish a breakdown of the total contract price showing the amount included therein for each principal category of the work, in such detail as requested, to provide a basis for determining process payments. In the preparation of estimates the Contracting Officer, at his discretion, may authorize material delivered on the site and preparatory work done to be taken into consideration. Material delivered to the Contractor at locations other than the site may also be taken into consideration (1) if such consideration is specifically authorized by the contract and (2) if the Contractor furnishes satisfactory evidence that he has acquired title to such material and that it will be utilized on the work covered by this contract.

(c) In making such progress payments, there shall be retained 10 percent of the estimated amount until final completion and acceptance of the contract work. However, if the Contracting Officer, at any time after 50 percent of the work has been completed, finds that satisfactory progress is being made, he may authorize any of the remaining progress payments to be made in full. Also, whenever the work is substantially complete, the Contracting Officer, if he considers the amount retained to be in excess of the amount adequate for the protection of the Government, at his discretion, may release to the Contractor all or a portion of such excess amount. Furthermore, on completion and acceptance of each separate building, public work, or other division of the contract, on which the price is stated separately in the contract, payment may be made therefor without retention of a percentage.

(d) All material and work covered by progress payments made shall thereupon become the sole property of the Government, but this provision shall not be construed as relieving the Contractor from the sole responsibility for all material and work upon which payments have been made or the restoration of any damaged work, or as waiving the right of the Government to require the fulfillment of all of the terms of the contract.

(e) Upon completion and acceptance of all work, the amount due the Contractor under this contract shall be paid upon the presentation of a properly executed voucher and after the Contractor shall have furnished the Government with a release, if required, of all claims against the Government arising by virtue of this contract, other than claims in stated amounts as may be specifically excepted by the Contractor from the operation of the release. If the Contractor's claim to amounts payable under the contract has been assigned under the Assignment of Claims Act of 1940, as amended (31 U.S.C. 203, 41 U.S.C. 15), a release may also be required of the assignee.

8. ASSIGNMENT OF CLAIMS

(a) Pursuant to the provisions of the Assignment of Claims Act of 1940, as amended (31 U.S.C. 203, 41 U.S.C. 15), if this contract provides for payments aggregating $1,000 or more, claims for moneys due or to become due the Contractor from the Government under this contract may be assigned to a bank, trust company, or other financing institution, including any Federal lending agency, and may thereafter be further assigned and reassigned to any such institution. Any such assignment or reassignment shall cover all amounts payable under this contract and not already paid, and shall not be made to more than one party, except that any such assignment or reassignment may be made to one party as agent or trustee for two or more parties participating in such financing. Unless otherwise provided in this contract, payments to an assignee of any moneys due or to become due under this contract shall not, to the extent provided in said Act, as amended, be subject to reduction or setoff. (The preceding sentence applies only if this contract is made in time of war or national emergency as defined in said Act; and is with the Department of Defense, the General Services Administration, the Atomic Energy Commission, the National Aeronautics and Space Administration, the Federal Aviation Agency, or any other department or agency of the United States designated by the President pursuant to Clause 4 of the proviso of section 1 of the Assignment of Claims Act of 1940, as amended by the Act of May 15, 1951, 65 Stat. 41.)

(b) In no event shall copies of this contract or of any plans, specifications, or other similar documents relating to work under this contract, if marked "Top Secret," "Secret," or "Confidential," be furnished to any assignee of any claim arising under this contract or to any other person not entitled to receive the same. However, a copy of any part or all of this contract so marked may be furnished, or any information contained therein may be disclosed, to such assignee upon the prior written authorization of the Contracting Officer.

9. MATERIAL AND WORKMANSHIP

(a) Unless otherwise specifically provided in this contract, all equipment, material, and articles incorporated in the work covered by this contract are to be new and of the most suitable grade for the purpose intended. Unless otherwise specifically provided in this contract, reference to any equipment, material, article, or patented process, by trade name, make, or catalog number, shall be regarded as establishing a standard of quality and shall not be construed as limiting competition, and the Contractor may, at his option, use any equipment, material, article, or process which, in the judgment of the Contracting Officer, is equal to that named. The Contractor shall furnish to the Contracting Officer for his approval the name of the manufacturer, the model number, and other identifying data and information respecting the performance, capacity, nature, and rating of the machinery and mechanical and other equipment which the Contractor contemplates incorporating in the work. When required by this contract or when called for by the Contracting Officer, the Contractor shall furnish the Contracting Officer for approval full information concerning the material or articles which he contemplates incorporating in the work. When so directed, samples shall be submitted for approval at the Contractor's expense, with all shipping charges prepaid. Machinery, equipment, material, and articles installed or used without required approval shall be at the risk of subsequent rejection.

(b) All work under this contract shall be performed in a skillful and workmanlike manner. The Contracting Officer may, in writing, require the Contractor to remove from the work any employee the Contracting Officer deems incompetent, careless, or otherwise objectionable.

10. Inspection and Acceptance

(a) Except as otherwise provided in this contract, inspection and test by the Government of material and workmanship required by this contract shall be made at reasonable times and at the site of the work, unless the Contracting Officer determines that such inspection or test of material which is to be incorporated in the work shall be made at the place of production, manufacture, or shipment of such material. To the extent specified by the Contracting Officer at the time of determining to make off-site inspection or test, such inspection or test shall be conclusive as to whether the material involved conforms to the contract requirements. Such offsite inspection or test shall not relieve the Contractor of responsibility for damage to or loss of the material prior to acceptance, nor in any way affect the continuing rights of the Government after acceptance of the completed work under the terms of paragraph (f) of this clause, except as hereinabove provided.

(b) The Contractor shall, without charge, replace any material or correct any workmanship found by the Government not to conform to the contract requirements; unless in the public interest the Government consents to accept such material or workmanship with an appropriate adjustment in contract price. The Contractor shall promptly segregate and remove rejected material from the premises.

(c) If the Contractor does not promptly replace rejected material or correct rejected workmanship, the Government (1) may, by contract or otherwise, replace such material or correct such workmanship and charge the cost thereof to the Contractor, or (2) may terminate the Contractor's right to proceed in accordance with Clause 5 of these General provisions.

(d) The Contractor shall furnish promptly, without additional charge, all facilities, labor, and material reasonably needed for performing such safe and convenient inspection and test as may be required by the Contracting Officer. All inspection and test by the Government shall be performed in such manner as not unnecessarily to delay the work. Special, full size, and performance tests shall be performed as described in this contract. The Contractor shall be charged with any additional cost of inspection when material and workmanship are not ready at the time specified by the Contractor for its inspection.

(e) Should it be considered necessary or advisable by the Government at any time before acceptance of the entire work to make an examination of work already completed, by removing or tearing out same, the Contractor shall, on request, promptly furnish all necessary facilities, labor, and material. If such work is found to be defective or nonconforming in any material respect, due to the fault of the Contractor or his subcontractors, he shall defray all the expenses of such examination and of satisfactory reconstruction. If, however, such work is found to meet the requirements of the contract, an equitable adjustment shall be made in the contract price to compensate the Contractor for the additional services involved in such examination and reconstruction and, if completion of the work has been delayed thereby, he shall, in addition, be granted a suitable extension of time.

(f) Unless otherwise provided in this contract, acceptance by the Government shall be made as promptly as practicable after completion and inspection of all work required by this contract. Acceptance shall be final and conclusive except as regards latent defects, fraud, or such gross mistakes as may amount to fraud, or as regards the Government's rights under any warranty or guarantee.

11. Superintendence By Contractor

The Contractor shall give his personal superintendence to the work or have a competent foreman or superintendent, satisfactory to the Contracting Officer, on the work at all times during progress, with authority to act for him.

12. Permits and Responsibilities

The Contractor shall, without additional expense to the Government, be responsible for obtaining any necessary licenses and permits, and for complying with any applicable Federal, State, and municipal laws, codes, and regulations, in connection with the prosecution of the work. He shall be similarly responsible for all damages to persons or property that occur as a result of his fault or negligence. He shall take proper safety and health precautions to protect the work, the workers, the public, and the property of others. He shall also be responsible for all materials delivered and work performed until completion and acceptance of the entire construction work, except for any completed unit of construction thereof which theretofore may have been accepted.

13. Conditions Affecting the Work

The Contractor shall be responsible for having taken steps reasonably necessary to ascertain the nature and location of the work, and the general and local conditions which can affect the work or the cost thereof. Any failure by the Contractor to do so will not relieve him from responsibility for successfully performing the work without additional expense to the Government. The Government assumes no responsibility for any understanding or representations concerning conditions made by any of its officers or agents prior to the execution of this contract, unless such understanding or representations by the Government are expressly stated in the contract.

14. Other Contracts

The Government may undertake or award other contracts for additional work, and the Contractor shall fully cooperate with such other contractors and Government employees and carefully fit his own work to such additional work as may be directed by the Contracting Officer. The Contractor shall not commit or permit any act which will interfere with the performance of work by any other contractor or by Government employees.

15. Patent Indemnity

Except as otherwise provided, the Contractor agrees to indemnify the Government and its officers, agents, and employees against liability, including costs and expenses, for infringement upon any Letters Patent of the United States (except Letters Patent issued upon an application which is now or may hereafter be, for reasons of national security, ordered by the Government to be kept secret or otherwise withheld from issue) arising out of the performance of this contract or out of the use or disposal by or for the account of the Government of supplies furnished or construction work performed hereunder.

16. Additional Bond Security

If any surety upon any bond furnished in connection with this contract becomes unacceptable to the Government, or if any such surety fails to furnish reports as to his financial condition from time to time as requested by the Government, the Contractor shall promptly furnish such additional security as may be required from time to time to protect the interests of the Government and of persons supplying labor or materials in the prosecution of the work contemplated by this contract.

17. Covenant Against Contingent Fees

The Contractor warrants that no person or selling agency has been employed or retained to solicit or secure this contract upon an agreement or understanding for a commission, percentage, brokerage, or contingent fee, excepting bona fide employees or bona fide established commercial or selling agencies maintained by the Contractor for the purpose of securing business. For breach or violation of this warranty the Government shall have the right to annul this contract without liability or in its discretion to deduct from the contract price or consideration, or otherwise recover, the full amount of such commission, percentage, brokerage, or contingent fee.

18. Officals Not To Benefit

No member of Congress or resident Commissioner shall be admitted to any share or part of this contract, or to any benefit that may arise therefrom; but this provision shall not be construed to extend to this contract if made with a corporation for its general benefit.

19. Buy American

(a) Agreement. In accordance with the Buy American Act (41 U.S.C. 10a—10d) and Executive Order 10582, December 17, 1954 (3 CFR Supp.), the Contractor agrees that only domestic construction material will be used (by the Contractor, subcontractors, materialmen, and suppliers) in the performance of this contract, except for nondomestic material listed in the contract.

(b)) Domestic construction material: "Construction material" means any article, material, or supply brought to the construction site for incorporation in the building or work. An unmanufactured construction material is a "domestic construction material" if it has been mined or produced in the United States. A manufactured construction material is a "domestic construction material" if it has been manufactured in the United States and if the cost of its components which have been mined, produced, or manufactured in the United States exceeds 50 percent of the cost of all its components. "Component" means any article, material, or supply directly incorporated in a construction material.

(c) Domestic component. A component shall be considered to have been "mined, produced, or manufactured in the United States" (regardless of its source in fact) if the article, material, or supply in which it is incorporated was manufactured in the United States and the component is of a class or kind determined by the Government to be not mined, produced, or manufactured in the United States in sufficient and reasonably available commercial quantities and of a satisfactory quality.

20. CONVICT LABOR

In connection with the performance of work under this contract, the Contractor agrees not to employ any person undergoing sentence of imprisonment at hard labor.

21. EQUAL OPPORTUNITY CLAUSE

(The following clause is applicable unless this contract is exempt under the rules and regulations of the President's Committee on Equal Employment Opportunity (41 CFT, Chapter 60). Exemptions include contracts and subcontracts (i) not exceeding $10,000, (ii) not exceeding $100,000 for standard commercial supplies or raw materials, and (iii) under which work is performed outside the United States and no recruitment of workers within the United States is involved.)

During the performance of this contract, the Contractor agrees as follows:

(a) The Contractor will not discriminate against any employee or applicant for employment because of race, creed, color, or national origin. The Contractor will take affirmative action to ensure that applicants are employed, and that employees are treated during employment, without regard to their race, creed, color, or national origin. Such action shall include, but not be limited to, the following: employment, upgrading, demotion or transfer; recruitment or recruitment advertising; layoff or termination; rates of pay or other forms of compensation; and selection for training, including apprenticeship. The Contractor agrees to post in conspicuous places, available to employees and applicants for employment, notices to be provided by the Contracting Officer setting forth the provisions of this nondiscrimination clause.

(b) The Contractor will, in all solicitations or advertisements for employees placed by or on behalf of the Contractor, state that all qualified applicants will receive consideration for employment without regard to race, creed, color, or national origin.

(c) The Contractor will send to each labor union or representative of workers with which he has a collective bargaining agreement or other contract or understanding, a notice, to be provided by the agency Contracting Officer, advising the said labor union or workers' representative of the Contractor's commitments under this nondiscrimination clause, and shall post copies of the notice in conspicuous places available to employees and applicants for employment.

(d) The Contractor will comply with all provisions of Executive Order No. 10925 of March 6, 1961, as amended, and of the rules, regulations, and relevant orders of the President's Committee on Equal Employment Opportunity created thereby.

(e) The Contractor will furnish all information and reports required by Executive Order No. 10925 of March 6, 1961, as amended, and by the rules, regulations, and orders of the said Committee, or pursuant thereto, and will permit access to his books, records, and accounts by the contracting agency and the Committee for purposes of investigation to ascertain compliance with such rules, regulations, and orders.

(f) In the event of the Contractor's noncompliance with the nondiscrimination clause of this contract or with any of the said rules, regulations, or orders, this contract may be canceled, terminated, or suspended in whole or in part and the Contractor may be declared ineligible for further Government contracts in accordance with procedures authorized in Executive Order No. 10925 of March 6, 1961, as amended, and such other sanctions may be imposed and remedies invoked as provided in the said Executive order or by rule, regulation, or order of the President's Committee on Equal Employment Opportunity, or as otherwise provided by law.

(g) The Contractor will include the provisions of paragraphs (a) through (g) in every subcontract or purchase order unless exempted by rules, regulations, or orders of the President's Committee on Equal Employment Opportunity issued pursuant to section 303 of Executive Order No. 10925 of March 6, 1961, as amended, so that such provisions will be binding upon each subcontractor or vendor. *The Contractor will take such action with respect to any subcontract or purchase order as the contracting agency may direct as a means of enforcing such provisions, including sanctions for noncompliance: Provided, however, that in the event the Contractor becomes involved in, or is threatened with, litigation with a subcontractor or vendor as a result of such direction by the contracting agency, the Contractor may request the United States to enter into such litigation to protect the interests of the United States.

*Unless otherwise provided, the Equal Opportunity Clause is not required to be inserted in subcontracts below the second tier except for subcontracts involving the performance of 'construction work' at the 'site of construction' (as those terms are defined in the Committee's rules and regulations) in which case the clause must be inserted in all such subcontracts. Subcontracts may incorporate by reference the Equal Opportunity Clause.

22. UTILIZATION OF SMALL BUSINESS CONCERNS

(a) It is the policy of the Government as declared by the Congress that a fair proportion of the purchases and contracts for supplies and services for the Government be placed with small business concerns.

(b) The Contractor agrees to accomplish the maximum amount of subcontracting to small business concerns that the Contractor finds to be consistent with the efficient performance of this contract.

Taken From
STANDARD FROM 32
JUNE 1964 EDITION
GENERAL SERVICES ADMINISTRATION
FED. PROC. REG. (41 CFT) 1-16.101

GENERAL PROVISIONS
(Supply Contract)

1. DEFINITIONS

As used throughout this contract, the following terms shall have the meaning set forth below:

   (a) The term "head of the agency" or "Secretary" means the Secretary, the Under Secretary, any Assistant Secretary, or any other head or assistant head of the executive or military department or other Federal agency; and the term "his duly authorized representative," means any person or persons or board (other than the Contracting Officer) authorized to act for the head of the agency or the Secretary.

   (b) The term "Contracting Officer" means the person executing this contract on behalf of the Government, and any other officer or civilian employee who is a properly designated Contracting Officer; and the term includes, except as otherwise provided in this contract, the authorized representative of a Contracting Officer acting within the limits of his authority.

   (c) Except as otherwise provided in this contract, the term "subcontracts" includes purchase orders under this contract.

2. CHANGES

The Contracting Officer may at any time, by a written order, and without notice to the sureties, make changes, within the general scope of this contract, in any one or more of the following: (i) Drawings, designs, or specifications, where the supplies to be furnished are to be specially manufactured for the Government in accordance therewith; (ii) method of shipment or packing; and (iii) place of delivery. If any such change causes an increase or decrease in the cost of, or the time required for, the performance of any part of the work under this contract, whether changed or not changed by any such order, an equitable adjustment shall be made in the contract price or delivery schedule, or both, and the contract shall be modified in writing accordingly. Any claim by the Contractor for adjustment under this clause must be asserted within 30 days from the date of receipt by the Contractor of the notification of change: *Provided, however,* That the Contracting Officer, if he decides that the facts justify such action, may receive and act upon any such claim asserted at any time prior to final payment under this contract. Where the cost of property made obsolete or excess as a result of a change is included in the Contractor's claim for adjustment, the Contracting Officer shall have the right to prescribe the manner of disposition of such property. Failure to agree to any adjustment shall be a dispute concerning a question of fact within the meaning of the clause of this contract entitled "Disputes." However, nothing in this clause shall excuse the Contractor from proceeding with the contract as changed.

3. EXTRAS

Except as otherwise provided in this contract, no payment for extras shall be made unless such extras and the price therefor have been authorized in writing by the Contracting Officer.

4. VARIATION IN QUANTITY

No variation in the quantity of any item called for by this contract will be accepted unless such variation has been caused by conditions of loading, shipping, or packing, or

142

allowances in manufacturing processes, and then only to the extent, if any, specified elsewhere in this contract.

5. INSPECTION

(a) All supplies (which term throughout this clause includes without limitation raw materials, components, intermediate assemblies, and end products) shall be subject to inspection and test by the Government, to the extent practicable at all times and places including the period of manufacture and in any event prior to acceptance.

(b) In case any supplies or lots of supplies are defective in material or workmanship or otherwise not in conformity with the requirements of this contract, the Government shall have the right either to reject them (with or without instructions as to their disposition) or to require their correction. Supplies or lots of supplies which have been rejected or required to be corrected shall be removed or, if permitted or required by the Contracting Officer, corrected in place by and at the expense of the Contractor promptly after notice, and shall not thereafter be tendered for acceptance unless the former rejection or requirement of correction is disclosed. If the Contractor fails promptly to remove such supplies or lots of supplies which are required to be removed, or promptly to replace or correct such supplies or lots of supplies, the Government either (i) may by contract or otherwise replace or correct such supplies and charge to the Contractor the cost occasioned the Government thereby, or (ii) may terminate this contract for default as provided in the clause of this contract entitled "Default." Unless the Contractor corrects or replaces such supplies within the delivery schedule, the Contracting Officer may require the delivery of such supplies at a reduction in price which is equitable under the circumstances. Failure to agree to such reduction of price shall be a dispute concerning a question of fact within the meaning of the clause of this contract entitled "Disputes."

(c) If any inspection or test is made by the Government on the premises of the Contractor or a subcontractor, the Contractor without additional charge shall provide all reasonable facilities and assistance for the safety and convenience of the Government inspectors in the performance of their duties. If Government inspection or test is made at a point other than the premises of the Contractor or a subcontractor, it shall be at the expense of the Government except as otherwise provided in this contract: *Provided,* That in case of rejection the Government shall not be liable for any reduction in value of samples used in connection with such inspection or test. All inspections and tests by the Government shall be performed in such a manner as not to unduly delay the work. The Government reserves the right to charge to the Contractor any additional cost of Government inspection and test when supplies are not ready at the time such inspection and test is requested by the Contractor or when reinspection or retest is necessitated by prior rejection. Acceptance or rejection of the supplies shall be made as promptly as practicable after delivery, except as otherwise provided in this contract; but failure to inspect and accept or reject supplies shall neither relieve the Contractor from responsibility for such supplies as are not in accordance with the contract requirements nor impose liability on the Government therefor.

(d) The inspection and test by the Government of any supplies or lots thereof does not relieve the Contractor from any responsibility regarding defects or other failures to meet the contract requirements which may be discovered prior to acceptance. Except as otherwise provided in this contract, acceptance shall be conclusive except as regards latent defects, fraud, or such gross mistakes as amount to fraud.

(e) The Contractor shall provide and maintain an inspection system acceptable to the Government covering the supplies hereunder. Records of an inspection work by the Contractor shall be kept complete and available to the Government during the performance of this contract and for such longer period as may be specified elsewhere in this contract.

6. RESPONSIBILITY FOR SUPPLIES

Except as otherwise provided in this contract, (i) the Contractor shall be responsible for the supplies covered by this contract until they are delivered at the designated delivery point, regardless of the point of inspection; (ii) after delivery to the Government at the designated point and prior to acceptance by the Government or rejection and giving notice

143

thereof by the Government, the Government shall be responsible for the loss or destruction of or damage to the supplies only if such loss, destruction, or damage results from the negligence of officers, agents, or employees of the Government acting within the scope of their employment; and (iii) the Contractor shall bear all risks as to rejected supplies after notice of rejection, except that the Government shall be responsible for the loss, or destruction of, or damage to the supplies only if such loss, destruction or damage results from the gross negligence of officers, agents, or employees of the Government acting within the scope of their employment.

7. PAYMENTS

The Contractor shall be paid, upon the submission of proper invoices or vouchers, the prices stipulated herein for supplies delivered and accepted or services rendered and accepted, less deductions, if any, as herein provided. Unless otherwise specified, payment will be made on partial deliveries accepted by the Government when the amount due on such deliveries so warrants; or, when requested by the Contractor, payment for accepted partial deliveries shall be made whenever such payment would equal or exceed either $1,000 or 50 percent of the total amount of this contract.

8. ASSIGNMENT OF CLAIMS

(a) Pursuant to the provisions of the Assignment of Claims Act of 1940, as amended (31 U.S.C. 203, 41 U.S.C. 15), if this contract provides for payments aggregating $1,000 or more, claims for moneys due or to become due the Contractor from the Government under this contract may be assigned to a bank, trust company, or other financing institution, including any Federal lending agency, and may thereafter be further assigned and reassigned to any such institution. Any such assignment or reassignment shall cover all amounts payable under this contract and not already paid, and shall not be made to more than one party, except that any such assignment or reassignment may be made to one party as agent or trustee for two or more parties participating in such financing. Unless otherwise provided in this contract, payments to an assignee of any moneys due or to become due under this contract shall not, to the extent provided in said Act, as amended, be subject to reduction or setoff. (The preceding sentence applies only if this contract is made in time of war or national emergency as defined in said Act and is with the Department of Defense, the General Services Administration, the Atomic Energy Commission, the National Aeronautics and Space Administration, the Federal Aviation Agency, or any other department or agency of the United States designated by the President pursuant to Clause 4 of the proviso of section 1 of the Assignment of Claims Act of 1940, as amended by the Act of May 15, 1951, 65 Stat. 41.)

(b) In no event shall copies of this contract or of any plans, specifications, or other similar documents relating to work under this contract, if marked "Top Secret," "Secret," or "Confidential," be furnished to any assignee of any claim arising under this contract or to any other person not entitled to receive the same. However, a copy of any part or all of this contract so marked may be furnished, or any information contained therein may be disclosed, to such assignee upon the prior wirtten authorization of the Contracting Officer.

9. ADDITIONAL BOND SECURITY

If any surety upon any bond furnished in connection with this contract becomes unacceptable to the Government or if any such surety fails to furnish reports as to his financial condition from time to time as requested by the Government, the Contractor shall promptly furnish such additional security as may be required from time to time to protect the interests of the Government and of persons supplying labor or materials in the prosecution of the work contemplated by this contract.

10. EXAMINATION OF RECORDS

(The following clause is applicable if the amount of this contract exceeds $2,500 and was entered into by means of negotiation, but is not applicable if this contract was entered into by means of formal advertising.)

(a) The Contractor agrees that the Comptroller General of the United States or any of his duly authorized representatives shall, until the expiration of three years after final

144

payment under this contract, have access to and the right to examine any directly pertinent books, documents, papers, and records of the Contractor involving transactions related to this contract.

(b) The Contractor further agrees to include in all his subcontracts hereunder a provision to the effect that the subcontractor agrees that the Comptroller General of the United States or any of his duly authorized representatives shall, until the expiration of three years after final payment under the subcontract, have access to and the right to examine any directly pertinent books, documents, papers, and records of such subcontractor, involving transactions related to the subcontract. The term "subcontract" as used in this clause excludes (i) purchase orders not exceeding $2,500 and (ii) subcontracts or purchase orders for public utility services at rates established for uniform applicability to the general public.

11. DEFAULT

(a) The Government may, subject to the provisions of paragraph (c) below, by written notice of default to the Contractor, terminate the whole or any part of this contract in any one of the following circumstnaces:

(i) If the Contractor fails to perform any of the other provisions of this contract, or so fails to make progress as to endanger performance of this contract in accordance with its terms, and in either of these two circumstances does not cure such failure within a period of 10 days (or such longer period as the Contracting Officer may authorize in writing) after receipt of notice from the Contracting Officer specifying such failure.

(b) In the event the Government terminates this contract in whole or in part as provided in paragraph (a) of this clause, the Government may procure, upon such terms and in such manner as the Contracting Officer may deem appropriate, supplies or services similar to those so terminated, and the Contractor shall be liable to the Government for any excess costs for such similar supplies or services: *Provided,* That the Contractor shall continue the performance of this contract to the extent not terminated under the provisions of this clause.

(c) Except with respect to defaults of subcontractors, the Contractor shall not be liable for any excess costs if the failure to perform the contract arises out of causes beyond the control and without the fault or negligence of the Contractor. Such causes may include, but are not restricted to, acts of God or of the public enemy, acts of the Government in either its sovereign or contractual capacity, fires, floods, epidemics, quarantine restrictions, strikes, freight embargoes, and unusually severe weather; but in every case the failure to perform must be beyond the control and without the fault or negligence of the Contractor. If the failure to perform is caused by the default of a subcontractor, and if such default arises out of causes beyond the control of both the Contractor and subcontractor, and without the fault or negligence of either of them, the Contractor shall not be liable for any excess costs for failure to perform, unless the supplies or services to be furnished by the subcontractor were obtainable from other sources in sufficient time to permit the Contractor to meet the required delivery schedule.

(d) If this contract is terminated as provided in paragraph (a) of this clause, the Government, in addition to any other rights provided in this clause, may require the Contractor to transfer title and deliver to the Government, in the manner and to the extent directed by the Contracting Officer, (i) any completed supplies, and (ii) such partially completed supplies and materials, parts, tools, dies, jigs, fixtures, plans, drawings, information, and contract rights (hereinafter called "manufacturing materials") as the Contractor has specifically produced or specifically acquired for the performance of such part of this contract as has been terminated; and the Contractor shall upon direction of the Contracting Officer. protect and preserve property in possession of the Contractor in which the Government has an interest. Payment for completed supplies delivered to and accepted by the Government shall be at the contract price. Payment for manufacturing materials delivered to and accepted by the Government and for the protection and preservation of property shall be in an amount agreed upon by the Contractor and Contracting Officer; failure to agree to such amount shall be a dispute concerning a question of fact within the meaning of the clause of this contract entitled "Disputes." The Government may withhold from amounts otherwise due the Contractor for such completed supplies or manufacturing materials such sum as the Contracting Officer determines to be necessary to protect the Government against loss because of outstanding liens or claims of former lien holders.

(e) If, after notice of termination of this contract under the provisions of this clause, it is determined for any reason that the Contractor was not in default under the provisions of this clause, or that the default was excusable under the provisions of this clause, the rights and obligations of the parties shall, if the contract contains a clause providing for termination for convenience of the Government, be the same as if the notice of termination had been issued pursuant to such clause. If, after notice of termination of this contract under the provisions of this clause, it is determined for any reason that the Contractor was not in default under the provisions of this clause, and if this contract does not contain a clause providing for termination for convenience of the Government, the contract shall be equitably adjusted to compensate for such termination and the contract modified accordingly; failure to agree to any such adjustment shall be a dispute concerning a question of fact within the meaning of the clause of this contract entitles "Disputes."

(f) The rights and remedies of the Government provided in this clause shall not be exclusive and are in addition to any other rights and remedies provided by law or under this contract.

12. DISPUTES

(a) Except as otherwise provided in this contract, any dispute concerning a question of fact arising under this contract which is not disposed of by agreement shall be decided by the Contracting Officer, who shall reduce his decision to writing and mail or otherwise furnish a copy thereof to the Contractor. The decision of the Contracting Officer shall be final conclusive unless, within 30 days from the date of receipt of such copy, the Contractor mails or otherwise furnishes to the Contracting Officer a written appeal addressed to the Secretary. The decision of the Secretary or his duly authorized representative for the determination of such appeals shall be final and conclusive unless determined by a court of competent jurisdiction to have been fraudulent, or capricious, or arbitrary, or so grossly erroneous as necessarily to imply bad faith, or not supported by substantial evidence. In connection with any appeal proceeding under this clause, the Contractor shall be afforded an opportunity to be heard and to offer evidence in support of its appeal. Pending final decision of a dispute hereunder, the Contractor shall proceed diligently with the performance of the contract and in accordance with the Contracting Officer's decision.

(b) This "Disputes" clause does not preclude consideration of law questions in connection with decisions provided for in paragraph (a) above: *Provided,* That nothing in this contract shall be construed as making final the decision of any administrative official, representative, or board on a question of law.

13. NOTICE AND ASSISTANCE REGARDING PATENT AND COPYRIGHT INFRINGEMENT

The provisions of this clause shall be applicable only if the amount of this contract exceeds $10,000.

(a) The Contractor shall report to the Contracting Officer, promptly and in reasonable written detail, each notice or claim of patent or copyright infringement based on the performance of this contract of which the Contractor has knowledge.

(b) In the event of any claim or suit against the Government on account of any alleged patent or copyright infringement arising out of the performance of this contract or out of the use of any supplies furnished or work or services performed hereunder, the Contractor shall furnish to the Government, when requested by the Contracting Officer, all evidence and information in possession of the Contractor pertaining to such suit or claim. Such evidence and information shall be furnished at the expense of the Government except where the Contractor has agreed to indemnify the Government.

14. BUY AMERICAN ACT

(a) In acquiring end products, the Buy American Act (41 U.S. Code 10 a-d) provides that the Government give preference to domestic source end products. For the purpose of this clause:

(i) "components" means those articles, materials, and supplies, which are directly incorporated in the end products;

(ii) "end products" means those articles, materials, and supplies, which are to be acquired under this contract for public use; and

(iii) a "domestic source end product" means (A) an unmanufactured end product which has been mined or produced in the United States and (B) an end product manufactured in the United States if the cost of the components thereof which are mined, produced, or manufactured in the United States exceeds 50 percent of the cost of all its components. For the purposes of this (a) (iii) (B), components of foreign origin of the same type or kind as the products referred to in (b) (ii) or (iii) of this clause shall be treated as components mined, produced, or manufactured in the United States.

(b) The Contractor agrees that there will be delivered under this contract only domestic source end products, except end products:

(i) which are for use outside the United States;

(ii) which the Government determines are not mined, produced, or manufactured in the United States in sufficient and reasonably available commercial quantities and of a satisfactory quality;

(iii) as to which the Secretary determines the domestic preference to be inconsistent with the public interest; or

(iv) as to which the Secretary determines the cost to the Government to be unreasonable.

(The foregoing requirements are administered in accordance with Executive Order No. 10582, dated December 17, 1954.)

15. Convict Labor

In connection with the performance of work under this contract, the Contractor agrees not to employ any person undergoing sentence of imprisonment at hard labor.

16. Contract Work Hours Standards Act—Overtime Compensation

This contract, to the extent that it is of a character specified in the Contract Work Hours Standards Act (40 U.S.C. 327–330), is subject to the following provisions and to all other applicable provisions and exceptions of such Act and the regulations of the Secretary of Labor thereunder.

(a) Overtime requirements. No Contractor or subcontractor contracting for any part of the contract work which may require or involve the employment of laborers or mechanics shall require or permit any laborer or mechanic in any workweek in which he is employed on such work to work in excess of eight hours in any calendar day or in excess of forty hours in such workweek on work subject to the provisions of the Contract Work Hours Standards Act unless such laborer or mechanic receives compensation at a rate not less than one and one-half times his basic rate of pay for all such hours worked in excess of eight hours in any calendar day or in excess of forty hours in such workweek, whichever is the greater number of overtime hours.

(b) Violation; liability for unpaid wages; liquidated damages. In the event of any violation of the provisions of paragraph (a), the Contractor and any subcontractor responsible therefor shall be liable to any affected employee for his unpaid wages. In addition, such Contractor and subcontractor shall be liable to the United States for liquidated damages. Such liquidated damages shall be computed with respect to each individual laborer or mechanic employed in violation of the provisions of paragraph (a) in the sum of $10 for each calendar day on which such employee was required or permitted to be employed on such work in excess of eight hours or in excess of his standard workweek of forty hours without payment of the overtime wages required by paragraph (a).

(c) Withholding for unpaid wages and liquidated damages. The Contracting Officer may withhold from the Government Prime Contractor, from any moneys payable on account of work performed by the Contractor or subcontractor, such sums as may administratively be determined to be necessary to satisfy any liabilities of such Contractor or subcontractor for unpaid wages and liquidated damages as provided in the provisions of paragraph (b).

147

(d) Subcontracts. The Contractor shall insert paragraphs (a) through (d) of this clause in all subcontracts, and shall require their inclusion in all subcontracts of any tier.

(e) Records. The Contractor shall maintain payroll records containing the information specified in 29 CFR 516.2(a). Such records shall be preserved for three years from the completion of the contract.

17. WALSH-HEALEY PUBLIC CONTRACTS ACT

If this contract is for the manufacture or furnishing of materials, supplies, articles, or equipment in an amount which exceeds or may exceed $10,000 and is otherwise subject to the Walsh-Healey Public Contracts Act, as amended (41 U.S. Code 35–45), there are hereby incorporated by reference all representations and stipulations required by said Act and regulations issued thereunder by the Secretary of Labor, such representations and stipulations being subject to all applicable rulings and interpretations of the Secretary of Labor which are now or may hereafter be in effect.

18. EQUAL OPPORTUNITY

(The following clause is applicable unless this contract is exempt under the rules and regulations of the President's Committee on Equal Employment Opportunity (41 CFR, Chapter 60). Exemptions include contracts and subcontracts (i) not exceeding $10,000, (ii) not exceeding $100,000 for standard commercial supplies or raw materials, and (iii) under which work is performed outside the United States and no recruitment of workers within the United States is involved.)

During the performance of this contract, the Contractor agrees as follows:

(a) The Contractor will not discriminate against any employee or applicant for employment because of race, creed, color, or national origin. The Contractor will take affirmative action to ensure that applicants are employed, and that employees are treated during employment, without regard to their race, creed, color, or national origin. Such action shall include, but not be limited to, the following: employment, upgrading, demotion or transfer; recruitment or recruitment advertising; layoff or termination; rates of pay or other forms of compensation; and selection for training, including apprenticeship. The Contractor agrees to post in conspicuous places, available to employees and applicants for employment, notices to be provided by the Contracting Officer setting forth the provisions of this nondiscrimination clause.

(b) The Contractor will, in all solicitations or advertisements for employees placed by or on behalf of the Contractor, state that all qualified applicants will receive consideration for employment without regard to race, creed, color, or national origin.

(c) The Contractor will send to each labor union or representative of workers with which he has a collective bargaining agreement or other contract or understanding, a notice, to be provided by the agency Contracting Officer, advising the said labor union or workers' representative of the Contractor's commitments under this nondiscrimination clause, and shall post copies of the notice in conspicuous places available to employees and applicants for employment.

(d) The Contractor will comply with all provisions of Executive Order No. 10925 of March 6, 1961, as amended, and of the rules, regulations, and relevant orders of the President's Committee on Equal Employment Opportunity created thereby.

(e) The Contractor will furnish all information and reports required by Executive Order No. 10925 of March 6, 1961, as amended, and by the rules, regulations, and orders of the said Committee, or pursuant thereto, and will permit access to his books, records, and accounts by the contracting agency and the Committee for purposes of investigation to ascertain compliance with such rules, regulations, and orders.

(f) In the event of the Contractor's noncompliance with the nondiscrimination clause of this contract or with any of the said rules, regulations, or orders, this contract may be canceled, terminated, or suspended in whole or in part and the Contractor may be declared ineligible for further Government contracts in accordance with procedures authorized in Executive Order No. 10925 of March 6, 1961, as amended, and such other sanctions may be imposed and remedies invoked as provided in the said Executive order or by rule, regulation, or order of the President's Committee on Equal Employment Opportunity, or as otherwise provided by law.

(g) The Contractor will include the provisions of paragraphs (a) through (g) in every subcontract or purchase order unless exempted by rules, regulations, or orders of the President's Committee on Equal Employment Opportunity issued pursuant to section 303 of Executive Order No. 10925 of March 6, 1961, as amended, so that such provisions will be binding upon each subcontractor or vendor.* The Contractor will take such action with respect to any subcontract or purchase order as the contracting agency may direct as a means of enforcing such provisions, including sanctions for noncompliance: Provided, however, that in the event the Contractor becomes involved in, or is threatened with, litigation with a subcontractor or vendor as a result of such direction by the contracting agency, the Contractor may request the United States to enter into such litigation to protect the interests of the United States.

Unless otherwise provided, the Equal Opportunity Clause is not required to be inserted in subcontracts below the second tier except for subcontracts involving the performance of 'construction work' at the 'site of construction' (as those terms are defined in the Committee's rules and regulations) in which case the clause must be inserted in all such subcontracts. Subcontracts may incorporate by reference the Equal Opportunity Clause.

19. OFFICIALS NOT TO BENEFIT

No member of or delegate to Congress, or resident Commissioner, shall be admitted to any share or part of this contract, or to any benefit that may arise therefrom; but this provision shall not be construed to extend to this contract if made with a corporation for its general benefit.

20. COVENANT AGAINST CONTINGENT FEES

The Contractor warrants that no person or selling agency has been employed or retained to solicit or secure this contract upon an agreement or understanding for a commission, percentage, brokerage, or contingent fee, excepting bona fide employees or bona fide established commercial or selling agencies maintained by the Contractor for the purpose of securing business. For breach or violation of this warranty the Government shall have the right to annul this contract without liability or in its discretion to deduct from the contract price or consideration, or otherwise recover, the full amount of such commission, percentage, brokerage, or contingent fee.

21. UTILIZATION OF SMALL BUSINESS CONCERNS

(a) It is the policy of the Government as declared by the Congress that a fair proportion of the purchases and contracts for supplies and services for the Government be placed with small business concerns.

(b) The Contractor agrees to accomplish the maximum amount of subcontracting to small business concerns that the Contractor finds to be consistent with the efficient performance of this contract.

22. UTILIZATION OF CONCERNS IN LABOR SURPLUS AREAS

(The following clause is applicable if this contract exceeds $5,000.)

It is the policy of the Government to place contracts with concerns which will perform such contracts substantially in areas of persistent or substantial labor surplus where this can be done, consistent with the efficient performance of the contract, at prices no higher than are obtainable elsewhere. The Contractor agrees to use his best effsorts to place his subcontracts in accordance with this policy. In complying with the foregoing and with paragraph (b) of the clause of this contract entitled "Utilization of Small Business Concerns," the Contractor in placing his subcontracts shall observe the following order of preference: (I) persistent labor surplus area concerns which are also small business concerns; (II) other persistent labor surplus area concerns; (III) substantial labor surplus area concerns which are also small business concerns; (IV) other substantial labor surplus area concerns; and (V) small business concerns which are not labor surplus area concerns.

| STANDARD FORM 33, JULY 1966
GENERAL SERVICES ADMINISTRATION
FED. PROC. REG. (41 CFR) 1-16.101 | SOLICITATION, OFFER,
AND AWARD | 3. CERTIFIED FOR NATIONAL DEFENSE UNDER
BDSA REG. 2 AND/OR DMS REG. 1.
RATING: | 4. PAGE
1 | OF |

1. CONTRACT (Proc. Inst. Ident.) NO.	2. SOLICITATION NO.		5. DATE ISSUED	6. REQUISITION/PURCHASE REQUEST NO.
	☐ ADVERTISED (IFB)	☐ NEGOTIATED (RFP)		

7. ISSUED BY	CODE	8. ADDRESS OFFER TO (If other than block 7)

SOLICITATION

9. Sealed offers in original and _____ copies for furnishing the supplies or services described in the Schedule will be received at the place specified in block 8, OR IF HAND-CARRIED, IN THE DEPOSITARY LOCATED IN _____ , until _____ .
(Time, Zone, and Date)

If this is an advertised solicitation, offers will be publicly opened at that time. CAUTION—LATE OFFERS. See par. 8 of Solicitation Instructions and Conditions. All offers are subject to the following:
1. The attached Solicitation Instructions and Conditions, SF 33A.
2. The General Provisions. SF 32 _____ edition, which is attached or incorporated herein by reference.

3. The Schedule included below and/or attached hereto.
4. Such other provisions, representations, certifications, and specifications as are attached or incorporated herein by reference. (Attachments are listed in the Schedule.)

FOR INFORMATION CALL (Name and Telephone No.) (No collect calls.):

SCHEDULE

10. ITEM NO.	11. SUPPLIES/SERVICES	12. QUANTITY	13. UNIT	14. UNIT PRICE	15. AMOUNT

OFFER (NOTE: Reverse Must Also Be Fully Completed By Offeror)

In compliance with the above, the undersigned offers and agrees, if this offer is accepted within _____ calendar days (60 calendar days unless a different period is inserted by the offeror) from the date for receipt of offers specified above, to furnish any or all items upon which prices are offered, at the price set opposite each item. delivered at the designated point(s), within the time specified in the Schedule.

16. DISCOUNT FOR PROMPT PAYMENT

_____ % 10 CALENDAR DAYS; _____ % 20 CALENDAR DAYS; _____ % 30 CALENDAR DAYS; _____ % _____ CALENDAR DAYS.

17. OFFEROR NAME & ADDRESS	CODE	FACILITY CODE	18. NAME AND TITLE OF PERSON AUTHORIZED TO SIGN OFFER (Type or Print)	
(Street, city, county, state, & ZIP Code) Area Code and Telephone No.: ☐ Check If Remittance Address Is Different From Above—Enter Such Address In Schedule.			19. SIGNATURE	20. OFFER DATE

AWARD (To Be Completed By Government)

21. ACCEPTED AS TO ITEMS NUMBERED	22. AMOUNT	23. ACCOUNTING AND APPROPRIATION DATA

24. SUBMIT INVOICES (4 copies unless otherwise specified) TO ADDRESS SHOWN IN BLOCK _____	25. NEGOTIATED PURSUANT TO:	☐ 10 U.S.C. 2304(a)( ) ☐ 41 U.S.C. 252(c)( )
26. ADMINISTERED BY CODE (If other than Block 7)	27. PAYMENT WILL BE MADE BY CODE	

28. NAME OF CONTRACTING OFFICER (Type or Print)	29 UNITED STATES OF AMERICA BY: _____ (Signature of Contracting Officer)	30. AWARD DATE

33-124   *Award will be made on this form. or on Standard Form 26. or by other official written notice.*

REPRESENTATIONS, CERTIFICATIONS, AND ACKNOWLEDGMENTS

The Offeror represents and certifies as part of his offer that: *(Check or complete all applicable boxes or blocks.)*

1. SMALL BUSINESS *(See par. 14 on SF 33A)*

He ☐ is, ☐ is not, a small business concern. If offeror is a small business concern and is not the manufacturer of the supplies offered, he also represents that all supplies to be furnished hereunder ☐ will, ☐ will not, be manufactured or produced by a small business concern in the United States, its possessions, or Puerto Rico.

2. REGULAR DEALER—MANUFACTURER *(Applicable only to supply contracts exceeding $10,000)*.

He is a ☐ regular dealer in, ☐ manufacturer of, the supplies offered.

3. CONTINGENT FEE *(See par. 15 on SF 33A)*

(a) He ☐ has, ☐ has not, employed or retained any company or person *(other than a full-time, bona fide employee working solely for the offeror)* to solicit or secure this contract, and (b) he ☐ has, ☐ has not, paid or agreed to pay any company or person *(other than a full-time, bona fide employee working solely for the offeror)* any fee, commission, percentage, or brokerage fee contingent upon or resulting from the award of this contract; and agrees to furnish information relating to (a) and (b) above, as requested by the Contracting Officer. *(For interpretation of the representation, including the term "bona fide employee," See Code of Federal Regulations, Title 41, Subpart 1-1.5.)*

4. TYPE OF BUSINESS ORGANIZATION

He operates as ☐ an individual, ☐ a partnership, ☐ a non profit organization, ☐ a corporation, incorporated under the laws of the State of _____

5. AFFILIATION AND IDENTIFYING DATA *(Applicable only to advertised solicitations.)*

Each offeror shall complete (a) and (b) if applicable, and (c) below:
(a) He ☐ is, ☐ is not, owned or controlled by a parent company. *(See par. 16 on SF 33A.)*
(b) If the offeror is owned or controlled by a parent company, he shall enter in the blocks below the name and main office address of the parent company:

NAME OF PARENT COMPANY	MAIN OFFICE ADDRESS *(Include ZIP code)*.

(c) Employer's Identification Number *(See par. 17 on SF 33A)*

OFFEROR'S E.I. NO.	PARENT COMPANY'S E.I. NO.

6. EQUAL OPPORTUNITY

He ☐ has, ☐ has not, participated in a previous contract or subcontract subject either to the Equal Opportunity clause herein or the clause originally contained in section 301 of Executive Order No. 10925, or the clause contained in section 201 of Executive Order No. 11114; that he ☐ has, ☐ has not, filed all required compliance reports; and that representations indicating submission of required compliance reports, signed by proposed subcontractors, will be obtained prior to subcontract awards. *(The above representation need not be submitted in connection with contracts or subcontracts which are exempt from the clause.)*

7. BUY AMERICAN CERTIFICATE

The offeror hereby certifies that each end product, except the end products listed below, is a domestic source end product (as defined in the *clause* entitled "Buy American Act"); and that components of unknown origin have been considered to have been mined, produced, or manufactured outside the United States.

EXCLUDED END PRODUCTS	COUNTRY OF ORIGIN

8. CERTIFICATION OF INDEPENDENT PRICE DETERMINATION *(See par. 18 on 33A.)*

(a) By submission of this offer, the offeror certifies, and in the case of a joint offer, each party thereto certifies as to its own organization, that in connection with this procurement:
(1) the prices in this offer have been arrived at independently, without consultation, communication, or agreement, for the purpose of restricting competition, as to any matter relating to such prices with any other offeror or with any competitor;
(2) unless otherwise required by law, the prices which have been quoted in this offer have not been knowingly disclosed by the offeror and will not knowingly be disclosed by the offeror prior to opening in the case of an advertised procurement or prior to award in the case of a negotiated procurement, directly or indirectly to any other offeror or to any competitor; and
(3) no attempt has been made or will be made by the offeror to induce any other person or firm to submit or not to submit an offer for the purpose of restricting competition.
(b) Each person signing this offer certifies that:
(1) he is the person in the offeror's organization responsible within that organization for the decision as to the prices being offered herein and that he has not participated, and will not participate, in any action contrary to (a) (1) through (a) (3) above; or
(2) (i) He is not the person in the offeror's organization responsible within that organization for the decision as to the prices being offered herein but that he has been authorized in writing to act as agent for the persons responsible for such decision in certifying that such persons have not participated, and will not participate, in any action contrary to (a) (1) through (a) (3) above, and as their agent does hereby so certify; and (ii) he has not participated, and will not participate, in any action contrary to (a) (1) through (a) (3) above.

ACKNOWLEDGMENT OF AMENDMENTS			
The offeror acknowledges receipt of amendments to the Solicitation for Offers and related documents numbered and dated as follows:			
AMENDMENT NO.	DATE	AMENDMENT NO.	DATE

NOTE.—*Offers must set forth full, accurate, and complete information as required by this Solicitation (including attachments). The penalty for making false statements in offers is prescribed in 18 U.S.C. 1001.*

Taken From
STANDARD FORM 33A, JULY 1966
GENERAL SERVICES ADMINISTRATION
FED. PROC. REG. (41 CFR) 1–16.101

SOLICITATION INSTRUCTIONS AND CONDITIONS

1. DEFINITIONS.
As used herein:

(a) The term "solicitation" means Invitation for Bids (IFB) where the procurement is advertised, and Request for Proposal (RFP) where the procurement is negotiated.

(b) The term "offer" means bid where the procurement is advertised, and proposal where the procurement is negotiated.

(c) For purposes of this solicitation and Block 2 of Standard Form 33, the term "advertised" includes Small Business Restricted Advertising and other types of restricted advertising.

2. PREPARATION OF OFFERS.
(a) Offerors are expected to examine the drawings, specifications, Schedule, and all instructions. Failure to do so will be at the offeror's risk.

(b) Each offeror shall furnish the information required by the solicitation. The offeror shall sign the solicitation and print or type his name on the Schedule and each Continuation Sheet thereof on which he makes an entry. Erasures or other changes must be initialed by the person signing the offer. Offers signed by an agent are to be accompanied by evidence of his authority unless such evidence has been previously furnished to the issuing office.

(c) Unit price for each unit offered shall be shown and such price shall include packing unless otherwise specified. A total shall be entered in the Amount column of the Schedule for each item offered. In case of discrepancy between a unit price and extended price, the unit price will be presumed to be correct, subject, however, to correction to the same extent and in the same manner as any other mistake.

(d) Offers for supplies or services other than those specified will not be considered unless authorized by the solicitation.

(e) Offeror must state a definite time for delivery of supplies or for performance of services unless otherwise specified in the solicitation.

(f) Time, if stated as a number of days, will include Saturdays, Sundays and holidays.

(g) Code boxes are for Government use only.

3. EXPLANATION TO OFFERORS.
Any explanation desired by an offeror regarding the meaning or interpretation of the solicitation, drawings, specifications, etc., must be requested in writing and with sufficient time allowed for a reply to reach offerors before the submission of their offers. Oral explanations or instructions given before the award of the contract will not be binding. Any information given to a prospective offeror concerning a solicitation will be furnished to all prospective offerors as an amendment of the solicitation, if such information is necessary to offerors in submitting offers on the solicitation or if the lack of such information would be prejudicial to uninformed offerors.

4. ACKNOWLEDGMENT OF AMENDMENTS TO SOLICITATIONS.
Receipt of an amendment to a solicitation by an offeror must be acknowledged (a) by signing and returning the amendment, (b) on the reverse of Standard Form 33, or (c) by letter or telegram. Such acknowledgment must be received prior to the hour and date specified for receipt of offers.

152

5. SUBMISSION OF OFFERS.

(a) Offers and modifications thereof shall be enclosed in sealed envelopes and addressed to the office specified in the solicitation. The offeror shall show the hour and date specified in the solicitation for receipt, the solicitation number, and the name and address of the offeror on the face of the envelope.

(b) Telegraphic offers will not be considered unless authorized by the solicitation; however, offers may be modified by telegraphic notice, provided such notice is received prior to the hour and date specified for receipt. (However, see par. 8.)

(c) Samples of items, when required, must be submitted within the time specified, and unless otherwise specified by the Government, at no expense to the Government. If not destroyed by testing, samples will be returned at offeror's request and expense, unless otherwise specified by the solicitation.

6. FAILURE TO SUBMIT OFFER.

If no offer is to be submitted, do not return the solicitation unless otherwise specified. A letter or postcard should be sent to the issuing office advising whether future solicitations for the type of supplies or services covered by this solicitation are desired. Failure of the recipient to offer, or to notify the issuing office that future solicitations are desired, may result in removal of the name of such recipient from the mailing list for the type of supplies or services covered by the solicitation.

7. MODIFICATION OR WITHDRAWAL OF OFFERS.

(a) If this solicitation is advertised, offers may be modified or withdrawn by written or telegraphic notice received prior to the exact hour and date specified for receipt of offers. An offer also may be withdrawn in person by an offeror or his authorized representative, provided his identity is made known and he signs a receipt for the offer, but only if the withdrawal is made prior to the exact hour and date set for receipt of offers. (However, see par. 8.)

(b) If this solicitation is negotiated, offers may be modified (subject to par. 8, when applicable) or withdrawn by written or telegraphic notice received at any time prior to award. Offers may be withdrawn in person by an offeror or his authorized representative, provided his identity is made known and he signs a receipt for the offer prior to award.

8. LATE OFFERS AND MODIFICATIONS OR WITHDRAWALS.

(This paragraph applies to all advertised solicitations. In the case of Department of Defense negotiated solicitations, it shall also apply to late offers and modifications (other than the normal revisions of offers by selected offerors during the usual conduct of negotiations with such offerors) but not to withdrawals of offers. Unless otherwise provided, this paragraph does not apply to negotiated solicitations issued by civilian agencies.)

(a) Offers and modifications of offers (or withdrawals thereof, if this solicitation is advertised) received at the office designated in the solicitation after the exact hour and date specified for receipt will not be considered unless: (1) they are received before award is made; and either (2) they are sent by registered mail, or by certified mail for which an official dated post office stamp (postmark) on the original Receipt for Certified Mail has been obtained, or by telegraph if authorized, and it is determined by the Government that the late receipt was due solely to delay in the mails, or delay by the telegraph company, for which the offeror was not responsible; or (3) if submitted by mail (or by telegram if authorized) it is determined by the Government that the late receipt was due solely to mishandling by the Government after receipt at the Government installation; provided, that timely receipt at such installation is established upon examination of an appropriate date or time stamp (if any) of such installation, or of other documentary evidence of receipt (if readily available) within the control of such installation or of the post office serving it. However, a modification of an offer which makes the terms of the otherwise successful offer more favorable to the Government will be considered at any time it is received and may thereafter be accepted.

(b) Offerors using certified mail are cautioned to obtain a Receipt for Certified Mail showing a legible, dated postmark and to retain such receipt against the chance that it will be required as evidence that a late offer was timely mailed.

(c) The time of mailing of late offers submitted by registered or certified mail shall be deemed to be the last minute of the date shown in the postmark on the registered mail receipt or registered mail wrapper or on the Receipt for Certified Mail unless the offeror furnishes evidence from the post office station of mailing which establishes an earlier time. In the case of certified mail, the only acceptable evidence is as follows: (1) where the Receipt for Certified Mail identifies the post office station of mailing, evidence furnished by the offeror which establishes that the business day of that station ended at an earlier time, in which case the time of mailing shall be deemed to be the last minute of the business day of that station; or (2) an entry in ink on the Receipt for Certified Mail showing the time of mailing and the initials of the postal employee receiving the item and making the entry, with appropriate written verification of such entry from the post office station of mailing, in which case the time of mailing shall be the time shown in the entry. If the postmark on the original Receipt for Certified Mail does not show a date, the offer shall not be considered.

9. DISCOUNTS. (a) Notwithstanding the fact that a blank is provided for a ten (10) day discount, prompt payment discounts offered for payment within less than twenty (20) calendar days will not be considered in evaluating offers for award, unless otherwise specified in the solicitation. However, offered discounts of less than 20 days will.be taken if payment is made within the discount period, even though not considered in the evaluation of offers.

(b) In connection with any discount offered, time will be computed from date of delivery of the supplies to carrier when delivery and acceptance are at point of origin, or from date of delivery at destination or port of embarkation when delivery and acceptance are at either of those points, or from the date correct invoice or voucher is received in the office specified by the Government, if the latter date is later than date of delivery. Payment is deemed to be made for the purpose of earning the discount on the date of mailing of the Government check.

10. AWARD OF CONTRACT. (a) The contract will be awarded to that responsible offeror whose offer conforming to the solicitation will be most advantageous to the Government, price and other factors considered.

(b) The Government reserves the right to reject any or all offers and to waive informalities and minor irregularities in offers received.

(c) The Government may accept any item or group of items of any offer, unless the offeror qualifies his offer by specific limitations. UNLESS OTHERWISE PROVIDED IN THE SCHEDULE, OFFERS MAY BE SUBMITTED FOR ANY QUANTITIIES LESS THAN THOSE SPECIFIED; AND THE GOVERNMENT RESERVES THE RIGHT TO MAKE AN AWARD ON ANY ITEM FOR A QUANTITY LESS THAN THE QUANTITY OFFERED AT THE UNIT PRICES OFFERED UNLESS THE OFFEROR SPECIFIES OTHERWISE IN HIS OFFER.

(d) A written award (or Acceptance of Offer) mailed (or otherwise furnished) to the successful offeror within the time for acceptance specified in the offer shall be deemed to result in a binding contract without further action by either party.

The following paragraphs (e) through (h) apply only to negotiated solicitations:

(e) The Government may accept within the time specified therein, any offer (or part thereof, as provided in (c) above), whether or not there are negotiations subsequent to its receipt, unless the offer is withdrawn by written notice received by the Government prior to award. If subsequent negotiations are conducted, they shall not constitute a rejection or counter offer on the part of the Government.

(f) The right is reserved to accept other than the lowest offer and to reject any or all offers.

(g) The Government may award a contract, based on initial offers received, without discussion of such offers. Accordingly, each initial offer should be submitted on the most

154

favorable terms from a price and technical standpoint which the offeror can submit to the Government.

(h) Any financial data submitted with any offer hereunder or any representation concerning facilities or financing will not form a part of any resulting contract; provided, however, that if the resulting contract contains a clause providing for price reduction for defective cost or pricing data, the contract price will be subject to reduction if cost or pricing data furnished hereunder is incomplete, inaccurate, or not current.

11. GOVERNMENT-FURNISHED PROPERTY. No material, labor, or facilities will be furnished by the Government unless otherwise provided for in the solicitation.

12. LABOR INFORMATION. General information regarding the requirements of the Walsh-Healey Public Contracts Act (41 U.S.C. 35–45), the Contract Work Hours Standards Act (40 U.S.C. 327–330), and the Service Contract Act of 1965 (41 U.S.C. 351–357) may be obtained from the Department of of Labor, Washington, D.C. 20210, or from any regional office of that agency. Requests for information should include the solicitation number, the name and address of the issuing agency, and a description of the supplies or services.

13. SELLER'S INVOICES. Invoices shall be prepared and submitted in quadruplicate (one copy shall be marked "original") unless otherwise specified. Invoices shall contain the following information: Contract and order number (if any), item numbers, description of supplies or services, sizes, quantities, unit prices, and extended totals. Bill of lading number and weight of shipment will be shown for shipments made on Government bills of lading.

14. SMALL BUSINESS CONCERN. A small business concern for the purpose of Government procurement is a concern, including its affiliates, which is independently owned and operated, is not dominant in the field of operation in which it is submitting offers on Government contracts, and can further qualify under the criteria concerning number of employees, average annual receipts, or other criteria, as prescribed by the Small Business Administration. (See Code of Federal Regulations, Title 13, Part 121, as amended, which contains detailed industry definitions and related procedures.)

15. CONTINGENT FEE. If the offeror, by checking the appropriate box provided therefor, has represented that he has employed or retained a company or person (other than a full-time bona fide employee working solely for the offeror) to solicit or secure this contract, or that he has paid or agreed to pay any fee, commission, percentage, or brokerage fee to any company or person contingent upon or resulting from the award of this contract, he shall furnish, in duplicate, a complete Standard Form 119, Contractor's Statement of Contingent or Other Fees. If offeror has previously furnished a completed Standard From 119 to the office issuing this solicitation, he may accompany his offer with a signed statement (a) indicating when such completed form was previously furnished, (b) identifying by number the previous solicitation or contract, if any, in connection with which such form was submitted, and (c) representing that the statement in such form is applicable to this offer.

16. PARENT COMPANY. A parent company for the purpose of this offer is a company which either owns or controls the activities and basic business policies of the offeror. To own another company means the parent company must own at least a majority (more than 50 percent) of the voting rights in the company. To control another company, such ownership is not required; if another company is able to formulate, determine, or veto basic business policy decisions of the offeror, such other company is considered the parent company of the offeror. This control may be exercised through the use of dominant minority voting rights, use of proxy voting, contractual arrangements, or otherwise.

17. EMPLOYER'S IDENTIFICATION NUMBER. (Applicable only to advertise solicitations.) The offeror shall insert in the applicable space on the offer form, if he has no parent company, his own Employer's Identification Number (E.I. No.) (Federal Social Security Number used on Employer's Quarterly Federal Tax Return, U.S. Treasury Department Form 941), or, if he has a parent company, the Employer's Identification Number of his parent company.

18. CERTIFICATION OF INDEPENDENT PRICE DETERMINATION. (a) This certification on the offer form is not applicable to a foreign offeror submitting an offer for a contract which requires performance or delivery outside the United States, its possessions, and Puerto Rico.

(b) An offer will not be considered for award where (a) (1), (a) (3), or (b) of the certification has been deleted or modified. Where (a)(2) of the certification has been deleted or modified, the offer will not be considered for award unless the offeror furnishes with the offer a signed statement which sets forth in detail the circumstances of the disclosure and the head of the agency, or his designee, determines that such disclosure was not made for the purpose of restricting competition.

19. ORDER OF PRECEDENCE. In the event of an inconsistency between provisions of this solicitation, the inconsistency shall be resolved by giving precedence in the following order: (a) the Schedule; (b) Solicitation Instructions and Conditions; (c) General Provisions; (d) other provisions of the contract, whether incorporated by reference or otherwise; and (e) the specifications.

STANDARD FORM 129 JANUARY 1966 EDITION FPR (41 CFR) 1-16.802	**BIDDER'S MAILING LIST APPLICATION**	INITIAL APPLICATION REVISION

Fill in all spaces. Insert "NA" in blocks not applicable. Type or print all entries. See reverse for instructions.

TO (Enter name and address of Federal agency to which form is submitted. Include ZIP code)	DATE

1. APPLICANT'S NAME AND ADDRESS (Include county and ZIP code)	2. ADDRESS (Include county and ZIP code) TO WHICH SOLICITATIONS ARE TO BE MAILED (If different from item 1)

3. TYPE OF ORGANIZATION (Check one)   **4. HOW LONG IN PRESENT BUSINESS**

INDIVIDUAL	PARTNERSHIP	NON-PROFIT ORGANIZATION

CORPORATION, INCORPORATED UNDER THE LAWS OF THE STATE OF

5. NAMES OF OFFICERS, OWNERS, OR PARTNERS

PRESIDENT	VICE PRESIDENT	SECRETARY
TREASURER	OWNERS OR PARTNERS	

6. AFFILIATES OF APPLICANT (Names, locations, and nature of affiliation. See definition on reverse)

7. PERSONS AUTHORIZED TO SIGN BIDS, OFFERS, AND CONTRACTS IN YOUR NAME (Indicate if agent)

NAME	OFFICIAL CAPACITY	TEL. NO. (Incl. area code)

8. IDENTIFY EQUIPMENT, SUPPLIES, MATERIALS, AND/OR SERVICES ON WHICH YOU DESIRE TO BID (See attached Federal agency's supplemental listing and instructions, if any)

9. TYPE OF BUSINESS (See definitions on reverse)

MANUFACTURER OR PRODUCER	REGULAR DEALER (Type 1)	REGULAR DEALER (Type 2)
SERVICE ESTABLISHMENT	CONSTRUCTION CONCERN	RESEARCH AND DEVELOPMENT FIRM

☐ SURPLUS DEALER (Check this box if you are also a dealer in surplus goods)

10. SIZE OF BUSINESS (See definitions on reverse)

SMALL BUSINESS CONCERN *	OTHER THAN SMALL BUSINESS CONCERN	
* If you are a small business concern, fill in (a) and (b):	(a) AVERAGE NUMBER OF EMPLOYEES (Including affiliates) FOR FOUR PRECEDING CALENDAR QUARTERS	(b) AVERAGE ANNUAL SALES OR RECEIPTS FOR PRECEDING THREE FISCAL YEARS

11. FLOOR SPACE (Square feet)		12. NET WORTH	
MANUFACTURING	WAREHOUSE	DATE	AMOUNT

13. SECURITY CLEARANCE (If applicable, check highest clearance authorized)

FOR	TOP SECRET	SECRET	CONFIDENTIAL	NAMES OF AGENCIES WHICH GRANTED SECURITY CLEARANCES (Include dates)
KEY PERSONNEL				
PLANT ONLY				

THIS SPACE FOR USE BY THE GOVERNMENT	**CERTIFICATION**
	I CERTIFY THAT INFORMATION SUPPLIED HEREIN (Including all pages attached) IS CORRECT AND THAT NEITHER THE APPLICANT NOR ANY PERSON (Or concern) IN ANY CONNECTION WITH THE APPLICANT AS A PRINCIPAL OR OFFICER, SO FAR AS IS KNOWN, IS NOW DEBARRED OR OTHERWISE DECLARED INELIGIBLE BY ANY AGENCY OF THE FEDERAL GOVERNMENT FROM BIDDING FOR FURNISHING MATERIALS, SUPPLIES, OR SERVICES TO THE GOVERNMENT OR ANY AGENCY THEREOF. SIGNATURE NAME AND TITLE OF PERSON AUTHORIZED TO SIGN (Type or print)

129-104

INFORMATION AND INSTRUCTIONS

Persons or concerns wishing to be added to a particular agency's bidder's mailing list for supplies or services shall file this properly completed and certified Bidder's Mailing List Application, together with such other lists as may be attached to the application form, with each procurement office of the Federal agency with which they desire to do business. If a Federal agency has attached a supplemental Commodity List with instructions, complete the application as instructed. Otherwise, identify in Item 8 the equipment, supplies, and/or services on which you desire to bid. *The application shall be submitted and signed by the principal as distinguished from an agent, however constituted.*

After placement on the bidder's mailing list of an agency, a supplier's failure to respond (*submission of bid, or notice in writing, that you are unable to bid on that particular transaction but wish to remain on the active bidder's mailing list for that particular item*) to Invitations for Bids will be understood by the agency to indicate lack of interest and concurrence in the removal of the supplier's name from the purchasing activity's bidder's mailing list for the items concerned.

TYPE OF BUSINESS DEFINITIONS
(See Item No. 9)

A. MANUFACTURER OR PRODUCER means a person (or concern) owning, operating, or maintaining a factory or establishment that produces, on the premises, the materials, supplies, articles, or equipment of the general character of those listed in Item No. 8, or in the Federal Agency's supplemental Commodity List, if attached.

B. REGULAR DEALER (Type 1) means a person (or concern) who owns, operates, or maintains a store, warehouse, or other establishment in which the materials, supplies, articles, or equipment of the general character listed in Item No. 8 or in the Federal Agency's supplemental Commodity List, if attached, are bought, kept in stock, and sold to the public in the usual course of business.

C. REGULAR DEALER (Type 2) in the case of supplies of particular kinds (*at present, petroleum, lumber and timber products, machine tools, raw cotton, green coffee, hay, grain, feed, or straw, agricultural liming materials, tea, raw or unmanufactured cotton linters*). "REGULAR DEALER" means a person (or concern) satisfying the requirements of the regulations (Code of Federal Regulations, Title 41, 50–201.101(b)) as amended from time to time, prescribed by the Secretary of Labor under the Walsh-Healey Public Contracts Act (Title 41 U.S. Code 35–45). For coal dealers, see Code of Federal Regulations, Title 41, 50–201.604(a).

D. SERVICE ESTABLISHMENT means a concern (or person) which owns, operates, or maintains any type of business which is principally engaged in the furnishing of nonpersonal services, such as (*but not limited to*) repairing, cleaning, redecorating, or rental of personal property, including the furnishing of necessary repair parts or other supplies as part of the services performed.

E. CONSTRUCTION CONCERN means a concern (or person) engaged in construction, alteration or repair (including dredging, excavating, and painting) of buildings, structures or other real property.

DEFINITIONS RELATING TO SIZE OF BUSINESS

A. SMALL BUSINESS CONCERN. A small business concern for the purpose of Government procurement is a concern, including its affiliates, which is independently owned and operated, is not dominant in the field of operation in which it is bidding on Government contracts and can further qualify under the criteria concerning number of employees, average annual receipts, or other criteria, as prescribed by the Small Business Administration. (See Code of Federal Regulations, Title 13, Part 121, as amended, which contains detailed industry definitions and related procedures.)

B. AFFILIATES. Business concerns are affiliates of each other when either directly or indirectly (i) one concern controls or has the power to control the other, or (ii) a third party controls or has the power to control both. In determining whether concerns are independently owned and operated and whether or not affiliation exists, consideration is given to all appropriate factors including common ownership, common management, and contractual relationship. (See Items Nos. 6 and 10.)

C. NUMBER OF EMPLOYEES. In connection with the determination of small business status, "number of employees" means the average employment of any concern, including the employees of its domestic and foreign affiliates, based on the number of persons employed on a full-time, part-time, temporary, or any other basis during the pay period ending nearest the last day of the third month in each calendar quarter for the preceding four quarters. If a concern has not been in existence for four full calendar quarters, "number of employees" means the average employment of such concern and its affiliates during the period such concern has been in existence based on the number of persons employed during the pay period ending nearest the last day of each month. (See Item No. 10.)

COMMERCE BUSINESS DAILY

The Commerce Business Daily, published by the Department of Commerce, contains information concerning proposed procurements, sales, and contract awards. For further information concerning this publication, contact your local Commerce Field Office.